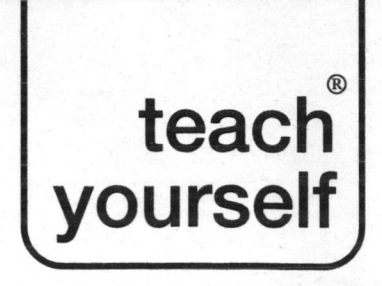

® teach yourself

your baby's development

teach® yourself

your baby's development
caroline deacon

For over 60 years, more than 50 million people have learnt over 750 subjects the **teach yourself** way, with impressive results.

be where you want to be
with **teach yourself**

For UK order enquiries: please contact Bookpoint Ltd, 130 Milton Park, Abingdon, Oxon, OX14 4SB. Telephone: +44 (0) 1235 827720. Fax: +44 (0) 1235 400454. Lines are open 09.00–17.00, Monday to Saturday, with a 24-hour message answering service. Details about our titles and how to order are available at www.teachyourself.co.uk.

For USA order enquiries: please contact McGraw-Hill Customer Services, PO Box 545, Blacklick, OH 43004-0545, USA. Telephone: 1-800-722-4726. Fax: 1-614-755-5645.

For Canada order enquiries: please contact McGraw-Hill Ryerson Ltd, 300 Water St, Whitby, Ontario L1N 9B6, Canada. Telephone: 905 430 5000. Fax: 905 430 5020.

Long renowned as the authoritative source for self-guided learning – with more than 50 million copies sold worldwide – the **teach yourself** series includes over 500 titles in the fields of languages, crafts, hobbies, business, computing and education.

British Library Cataloguing in Publication Data: a catalogue record for this title is available from the British Library.

Library of Congress Catalog Card Number: on file.

First published in UK 2007 by Hodder Education, 338 Euston Road, London, NW1 3BH.

First published in US 2007 by The McGraw-Hill Companies, Inc.

This edition published 2007.

The **teach yourself** name is a registered trade mark of Hodder Headline.

Copyright © 2007 Caroline Deacon

Typeset by Transet Limited, Coventry, England.
Printed in Great Britain for Hodder Education, a division of Hodder Headline, an Hachette Livre UK Company, 338 Euston Road, London, NW1 3BH, by Cox & Wyman Ltd, Reading, Berkshire.

The publisher has used its best endeavours to ensure that the URLs for external websites referred to in this book are correct and active at the time of going to press. However, the publisher and the author have no responsibility for the websites and can make no guarantee that a site will remain live or that the content will remain relevant, decent or appropriate.

Hachette's policy is to use papers that are natural, renewable and recyclable products and made from wood grown in sustainable forests. The logging and manufacturing processes are expected to conform to the environmental regulations of the country of origin.

Impression number   10 9 8 7 6 5 4 3 2 1
Year   2012 2011 2010 2009 2008 2007

contents

dedication

To my children – Alasdair, Chris and Josie.

acknowledgements

Despite gaining a degree in psychology long before I had children, all that I had learnt went out of my head when I became a mother, and instead I adopted the seat of the pants approach to parenting. As each seemingly insurmountable problem occurred, the amount of contradictory advice we received was amazing, and we stumbled along trying one thing then another while our children carried on providing us with suitably challenging scenarios.

I began to think that I was fortunate that so far our children have not turned out to be delinquent, disturbed or damaged by our continual experiments in parenting, though they might well disagree with me!

However, in revisiting all that I had learnt in those heady days as an undergraduate in order to produce this book, I was quite pleased to see that some of the things I had learnt must have sunk in, even if unconsciously, and for that I would like to thank the University of Edinburgh's Department of Psychology. That is not to say that they are responsible for any mistakes in this book – any errors are entirely my own.

I do also have to thank my mother, Janet King, who sparked an interest in psychology in the first place by filling her house with books by people like R. D. Laing, Carl Jung and others. I think my father, John Wheaton, was disappointed that I did not become a 'proper' scientist like an engineer or physicist; I hope that this book goes some way to making up for it.

Above all though, I would like to thank my husband Mark, and my three children Alasdair, Chris and Josie for once again showing endless patience as I closeted myself in my study to produce this book.

Caroline Deacon

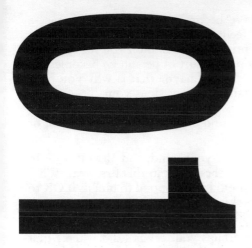

introduction

In this chapter you will learn:
- why this book will help you look after your baby
- whether your baby is generally pre-programmed
- how far you can influence your baby's development.

Congratulations! You have become, or about to become, a parent. You are probably feeling excited, but also quite nervous – a new human being is entirely dependent on you for survival. How he grows and develops, the sort of person he becomes, all this might be down to you. And maybe that is why you have bought this book. You want to know, does your input really matter? Will your baby grow up to become an accountant, a rock star, a famous artist or a notorious criminal because of or in spite of what you do?

Or maybe that had not crossed your mind, and all you want to know is how to get off to the best start in this first year. What will your baby need, how should you respond to him, is it OK to leave him to cry? Or will picking him up each time he cries, teach him to be attention-seeking?

Then on the other hand, perhaps you feel as I did when I first had a baby; where is the manual? What am I supposed to do? What on earth does it mean when he cries? If he smiles, is it just wind, or does he really know who I am? Is it OK if I go back to work early? Do I really have to play with him when he's only a baby, or read him a book, or could I just put him in front of the TV and let that entertain him? After all he's not going to remember any of this, is he?

Hopefully this book will answer all these questions, and do more besides. I hope it will give you confidence in your ability to parent this new human being, and that it will tell you that what you feel like doing is actually the right thing to do, but will also explain why it is right.

Why you are important to your baby

In the course of this book you will discover that the most important things you can provide for a baby in his first year are love and interaction. Love will actually help your baby to grow, lack of love will stunt him, as you will see. Interaction, of course, springs from love; you will talk to and interact with your baby because you love him and because loving someone means wanting to be with them, relating to them. And, as it happens, the most stimulating thing you can do for your baby in this first year is to interact with him; this will help him learn, form connections in his brain, and it will also teach him how to speak and eventually communicate with the world into which he has been born. This book will show you why interaction is important, and more importantly how to interact with your baby in a positive and helpful way.

Throughout this book, you will see that although your baby is born very capable, he depends utterly on your involvement to grow and develop. You will discover that the most important gift he has is to be flexible – he can adapt to any language, any society. This flexibility has made human beings the dominant species on the planet, able to survive in any environment. Babies fit into this by being good at learning, excellent imitators and taking many years to mature. The only resources they need are adults around them who want to help them learn.

In fact, finding out how your baby develops will also tell you quite a lot about how the human race works and why we all behave as we do, which is why psychologists spend such a lot of time looking at babies, at least they have done recently, because throughout most of history, babies were simply thought of as little adults; no one considered studying them for their own sake until the twentieth century when we realized that if we want to understand how human beings work, taking a look at how we get going in the first place might shed some light on the subject.

If we want to understand how people solve problems for instance, why not look at how babies tackle shape sorters? If we want to understand how language works, perhaps studying how babies learn to speak would be revealing. So for the last 100 years or so, psychologists have devoted their lives to studying how babies develop and, in the course of their studies, they have revealed much about human nature in general. Now you as parents can benefit from this body of knowledge, finding out what your baby is doing at each stage in his life, and why.

Can you influence the way your baby turns out?

Some fairly fundamental questions have vexed psychologists, philosophers and others, which we often refer to as the 'nature versus nurture' divide:

• Are babies pre-programmed to behave in a certain way, or do they learn from their parents and the society in which they live?
• Are human beings ruled by instincts that were created by the forces of evolution, or are such primitive drives irrelevant in the modern-day world?

- As adults, are we at the mercy of unconscious impulses created by our early childhood experiences, or are we instead driven by equally unconscious, biologically pre-determined neural or chemical impulses?
- And most importantly, what effect does all this have on how we raise our children?

Traditionally psychologists were split into two camps: empiricists and nativists. Empiricists said that babies are born like 'blank slates waiting to be written on'; that for a newborn baby, the world is a 'blooming, buzzing confusion', so that babies need to learn everything from scratch. Nativists on the other hand, believed that we are actually born with lots of innate capabilities, which means, of course, that babies have less to learn, instead they simply wait for things to unfold, their development all being genetically pre-determined.

In some ways you could say that empiricists are optimistic about human behaviour – if nothing is pre-ordained then, with the right environment, every baby could potentially grow up to be Einstein, while nativists are more pessimistic; if everything is innate, then there is not much potential for change. And the question is very important; if we discover that every baby's behaviour is governed by their genes, then there is no point in putting public money into helping underprivileged children: in fact we could probably just screen out undesirable children before they were born by reading off their genes like a supermarket barcode. Less dramatically, and of more relevance to you, it would also mean that you would not really have to do much to help your baby develop, as everything would just happen at the right stage as an automatic process.

If babies did develop according to a set of genetic instructions, then their early behaviour would be mostly instinctive (see box below). The problem for psychologists is that it's really difficult to work out what is instinctive and what has been learnt. While a behaviour that's already present at birth might look as if it's instinctive, in fact babies actually have nine months of learning before they are born, i.e. in utero. So for instance at birth your baby will respond to his mother's voice, preferring it to other female voices, but this of course is because he has *learnt* to recognize it; nothing to do with instinct.

> **Definition of instinctive behaviour**
>
> An instinct is a behaviour that is a product of evolution, and as such is shared by all members of the species. It is present at birth or develops at a particular stage in an animal's life (instinctive sexual behaviour might appear at puberty for instance). Any differences between individuals are thus due to differences in the genes.

Even when behaviour is instinctive, it can change with experience. For instance, newly hatched baby gulls immediately begin to peck at their parent's bill to elicit food, so this is an instinct (they cannot have learnt that this behaviour will produce food) but over time the chicks get more accurate at pecking, so they are learning from experience.

A similar thing happens with smiling; human babies all start to smile at around five weeks *even if they are blind*, so this must be an instinct (blind babies cannot be copying their parents) but as time goes on, babies who can see develop a wide repertoire of smiles, while blind children become less responsive and their facial expressions become more static with time. So smiling is an innate behaviour, but experience modifies this behaviour.

What we should conclude from these few examples and many more besides, is that neither empiricists nor nativists are right; instead there is an interaction between genetics and environment, so a particular behaviour could be instinctive – your baby is born to do it, but he will then change that behaviour with experience.

In fact we now know that this interaction between genes and environment starts happening from the minute the egg that will become your baby, is fertilized. The way he develops in the womb follows a very clear pattern, so there are strong genetic instructions at work here, but the environment of the womb can have a profound effect too, which is why pregnant women have to be so careful about their diets.

As an example, teratogens are environmental factors which create developmental abnormalities in the foetus leading to birth defects. One terrible such teratogen was the drug Thalidomide. Prescribed to mothers in the 1950s to combat morning sickness, unfortunately, if it was taken during the first two months of pregnancy, it resulted in babies being born with severe limb deformities. Drugs such as heroin, cocaine, alcohol and nicotine are all teratogens as they can all affect a baby's development in the womb, as can poor nutrition, infectious diseases such as rubella and chickenpox, and maternal stress.

Fascinating fact
Pregnancy sickness evolved to protect your baby.
Some foods, which are fine for women to eat under normal circumstances, can harm foetuses. The first three months after conception, when the major organs are forming, is a particularly vulnerable time, as we can see from Thalidomide above. And this is the time when morning sickness is at its worst, the effect being to severely curtail what the mother will eat, even if she's unaware she's pregnant. Interestingly women who do have morning sickness are less likely to miscarry.

What we shall see in this book is that babies are born with a wide range of innate abilities – genetic pre-programming if you like – but that they can also learn incredibly rapidly. In fact having these inborn capacities is *precisely* what allows them to learn so quickly from their environment, and throughout this book you will find out that there are ways to help your baby maximize his genetic potential by providing just the right environment for him at each stage.

We shall also see that your baby's development is not only an interaction between genes and environment but also a moving between what psychologists call 'specificity' and 'plasticity'. Plasticity refers to the fact that there is a great deal of flexibility in development; so that even though your baby's brain is born with some specific instructions to follow (specificity), it is through interacting with people, through participating in the culture and the physical world, that his brain is actually constructed. Like a flatpack piece of furniture, our genes provide a starter kit and a basic 'how to' manual to build a brain, but the world around us picks up where our genes cannot, causing the connections in the brain to form as your baby progresses from embryo to infancy and beyond.

How this book works

Having a new baby to look after means that time is the one thing you don't have, so this book is organized in such a way that you don't need to read it all, cover to cover, to find out what you need.

Section One is for parents who want to know what their baby is doing at each stage of development and why. It starts with an overview of how your baby gets moving and the stages he needs to go through in the first year. Then it breaks down into age groups: Chapter 03 looks at what is happening for your baby in his first six weeks, when your baby is getting used to the world and coming to terms with the input from his senses; Chapter 04 looks at six weeks to six months, when your baby is still relatively helpless, is struggling to control his body, but when he is now more alert and ready to interact with you; and Chapter 05 takes you from six months to toddlerhood, basically from sitting to walking. Each of these three chapters will look at how the world appears from your baby's point of view at that stage, and knowing this will help you respond appropriately. At each stage, therefore, you will find out how you can comfort your baby, how you should respond to his crying and why. You will also discover how to interact with your baby in an age appropriate way, thus stimulating him and helping him onto the next stage of development.

Section Two covers special situations like premature babies or twins and multiple births, so if you have a full-term singleton baby you can skip this part.

Section Three will then explain in more detail why love and interaction are important for your baby. It will look at how your baby's brain grows and how this is affected by your input. Part One of this section looks at how your baby bonds with you and with other members of his family, as well as how these early relationships affect your baby's sense of security, both now and as he grows up. We look too at the implications of this for childcare, and what the best sort of childcare might be if you have to leave your baby to return to work. We explore a bit more about your baby's place in the family – how different family structures work for your baby, his relationship to siblings – and at the same time, we look at how your baby might affect your relationship with your partner, how to maintain that relationship, and the effect on your baby if the relationship breaks down. We also look into the future to make some

9

suggestions about how your approach to parenting might change as your baby grows up.

Part Two of this section continues to look at how your baby's brain grows and how it is affected by your input, but here the emphasis is on your baby learning about the world. So firstly we look at how your baby learns, how he organizes his knowledge and why, and then we look at how he learns to communicate and eventually to speak. Finally we look at whether play matters for a baby, what play means and how to play with your baby, and whether boys and girls develop differently.

You should find that you can read the part of the book which interests you most at any time, and hopefully you will find it easy to read and understand, and above all that you can put it into practice with your baby. Enjoy!

Case study

Daniel has just been born, and his parents, Ann and Brian are gazing at him in amazement. Brian comments on his long fingers and toes, and this starts Ann wondering what else they might discover as time unfolds, because Ann is adopted, and she has no contact with her birth mother.

Ann will probably find that she thinks far more about her genetic inheritance now that she has a baby, but unless Daniel has inherited one of a few very rare and very particular genetic abnormalities, there is no real need for her to know any more than she does already.

How Daniel turns out will depend partly on his genes, but far more important will be the environment she and Brian create for him. If it is a loving home, with consistent parenting and plenty of stimulation, he will grow up just fine.

Summary of this chapter

- The most important things a baby needs in his first year are love and interaction.
- If you believe that everything is inborn and genetically determined, then it would not really matter what you did, your baby would turn out in a particular way because his genes directed him to do so.

- In fact it is very hard to separate out what is inborn, instinctual behaviour that all babies will do, and what is actually learnt.
- We now believe though, that your baby is a product of an interaction between his genes and the environment you provide, and that providing the right environment will allow him to fulfil his genetic potential.

What this means for you and your baby

It might seem incredibly daunting, that you are responsible for providing the right environment for your baby's development. The good news is that your baby will guide you in what he needs, as you will see. He loves to learn, and will complain if he gets bored. Learning is as natural to him as feeding or breathing. In addition this book will show you that adults instinctively change their behaviour to provide exactly what a baby needs. So don't get too concerned about what you need to do; your baby will develop normally if you give him your love and your time.

section one

one
your step-by-step guide to your baby's development

Introduction

In this section, you can find out what to expect from your baby at each stage of development. The aim of this section of the book is for you to understand what your baby might be doing at any particular age, how he is growing physically and mentally and how to interact with your baby in an appropriately stimulating way, as well as being able to calm and settle your baby by understanding why he is crying and how the world appears from his point of view. This section is very much concentrating on 'what' rather than 'why'; later parts of the book will focus on explaining why your baby is doing what he is doing, and will give you a more theoretical understanding of how your baby develops overall.

As you saw in Chapter 01, your baby's development unfolds as an interaction between his genes and his environment. His genes tell him what to do and roughly when to do it, but the fine tuning of his skills happens in an environment that consists mainly of you.

This means that your input is important; you need to be there to comfort him, to interact with him, to support and entertain him. But there is no need to be anxious about this: Firstly your baby wants to develop, and he will be leading the way to some extent. Secondly you will find that you do know what to do as long as you are prepared to put in the time and effort to be with your baby and to follow his lead, i.e. his cues.

Having said that, while you may want to help your baby develop, and although there is always plenty that you can do, it is worth remembering that you cannot skip stages. Your baby has to learn to sit before he can stand, crawl before he can walk. Some things will be impossible for him to do until his brain is ready. For instance being able to speak depends on his mouth enlarging, his palate becoming arched and tongue smaller, which will happen somewhere between 24 and 36 weeks. Before that he will not be able to form words. We therefore start this section with an overview of how your baby develops physically in this first year, in other words, how he gets moving.

In addition, sometimes your baby will seem to grasp a skill and then lose it again. This is perfectly normal; as different skills develop they compete for the brain's energy and so the focus of the brain's energy shifts. His brain needs to consolidate acquired skills so development often happens in spurts.

Your baby will make tremendous physical progress in his first year, and there is plenty you can do to help him along, as we shall see.

02

getting moving – how your baby develops physically in the first year

In this chapter you will learn:
- why it takes your baby such a long time to get moving
- that carrying your baby may help her development
- how your baby learns to use her hands to manipulate objects.

For your baby to really take part in her physical world, to interact on her own terms with the things she finds around herself, she will need:

- to gain control over her body so that she can move herself around by crawling or walking
- to develop control over her hands in order to pick up and manipulate objects.

Yet it will take most of her first year to really master these tasks. Why does it take so long?

What your baby can already do at birth

Although your baby is born completely helpless, she can control some important muscles, particularly those that help her communicate, namely the small muscles in her face. At birth she will frown, attempt to copy your facial expressions; she can even deliberately stick out her tongue to imitate you. But it will take her a few weeks to refine these facial expressions so she can make different types of smiles, and even longer to gain control over her arms and hands, while controlling all the large muscles in her body so she can balance and walk will take at least a year.

Although you might feel desperate at times to help your baby get moving, especially when she is trying to sit up or crawl and is getting frustrated, it is worth realizing that while you can certainly empathize and be as much help as you can, the frustration she is feeling is not only perfectly normal but is also probably motivating her to progress!

The other point to note is that physical development bears very little relationship to intellectual development, so even if your child is the last one in her circle to crawl or walk, it does not mean she will be less intelligent than her peers.

Getting moving – controlling the large muscles

In order to really get around the world, your baby is going to need to sit up, crawl and then walk. This means developing strength in her neck and back muscles to support her head and spine, which will take several months, with muscle control developing top down, i.e. neck to bottom.

The problem is that in the weightlessness of the womb there is little opportunity to strengthen muscles, so when she is first born her head, which in relation to her body is much larger than ours, is just too heavy for the muscles of her back and neck. She will immediately start to work these muscles to strengthen them, and if you hold her against your shoulder you will feel her lifting her head away from you in tiny little jerks, just as if she is deliberately bumping against you – this is her practising head control.

Therefore holding your baby upright against you when winding her or simply cuddling or comforting her, also gives her an opportunity to strengthen her neck muscles.

After a few weeks she is strong enough to hold her head away from you for a few minutes at a time as long as you are stationary, but if you are moving about she will just not be able to steady herself enough.

By about ten weeks she will have mastered control over her neck and can keep her head and neck steady in most conditions; now it will be her shoulders that let her down. In fact, working down her back like this, she will not gain full control of her whole spine until at she is at least six months old – the earliest she might begin to be able to sit up unaided.

- Put her on her tummy at least once a day to let her practise holding her head up.
- Although babies should not sleep on their front, it is important they spend some waking time each day on their tummies to help strengthen their necks.
- Don't sit your baby in her car seat except when she is actually travelling, as she will be too hunched over and will not be able to move her limbs freely.

As she steadily gains control over her head, her body also becomes unclenched from that foetal position she is initially so fond of, and she will begin to straighten her arms and legs (her hands will unclench too so she can start to grasp things voluntarily – see below). Once this happens, she can start to practise her leg movements; by about 12 weeks of age she will love lying on her back kicking.

- As your baby starts to unfurl, give her some time each day lying on her back on the floor with her nappy off.
- Once she starts to enjoy kicking, then put her on a variety of surfaces so she can experience different textures.
- Tie a helium balloon to her ankle and see what she does!

By the age of four or five months, when she is on her tummy she may be able to raise her head *or* raise her bottom into the air, but not both at the same time. Some babies even manage to work their way across the floor by alternating head and bottom raising, but this is not true crawling. To really crawl she needs to get onto her hands and knees, and this won't happen till she is about seven or eight months.

The first time she crawls she may actually go backwards – very frustrating indeed – but within a few days she should figure it out.

Put a toy just out of her reach so she has something to aim for.

Walking is much harder to accomplish – not surprising really as our ancestors basically adapted a skeleton which was designed to go on all fours. That's probably why so many of us have back problems in life; it would really have been far more efficient to remain as we were!

But your baby is driven to walk, and once she has developed the control right down the spine to her bottom and can sit up, it won't be long till she's able to stand. First she needs to keep her knees stiff; then she has to get hips under control (so this part of the process is not top to toe in fact). Because, as with every physical skill, practice is important, there will be several weeks of her pulling herself to a standing position using whatever is available (chairs, table legs, even your hair if it's in reach). Sometimes when she gets there, she will not be able to get down and will wail for help. Despite the padded bottom it's a bit scary to just bend your knees and let go!

Sitting up

In order to sit up, your baby needs to develop strength and co-ordination in all her muscles through her back and bottom. This develops top down:

- **At birth** she can't support the weight of her head, so you will have to help her.

  At first, support your baby by resting her neck and shoulders on your forearm; she will not like having the back of her head held. Alternatively hold her upright tummy to your tummy so her head is level with the top of your shoulders.

- **By two months**, her neck is stronger. If you put her on her tummy, she will briefly lift her head and have a look around.

  You can help her practise this by putting her on her tummy for a few minutes each day.

- **At three months** head control has improved, and she loves to be held upright so she gets a new and interesting perspective on the world. This keeps her awake too, as babies lying down are more likely to doze off.

  This is the time to try a good supportive doorway bouncer. Make sure she can only just contact the ground with tiptoes, otherwise she may bounce too hard on her feet.

- **At six months** she enjoys rolling over, and may be able to sit up for periods of time, depending how stable her lumbar region is. Rolling over is the first step to moving around the world, and you may see her figuring out a rolling strategy for reaching something she wants.

  Sit her with cushions back and side, and put a variety of objects directly in front of her to examine and play with.

Gaining balance – why the vestibular system is so important to babies

While all this muscle control development is developing, another system is also maturing which is crucial to getting moving: balance.

The vestibular system is the oldest of our sensory systems; it's believed to have evolved around 0.6 billion years ago. We rely on receptors in the inner ear to sense any changes of our position in space; more specifically any movement of the head in space. Our muscles and joints also contribute to our awareness of where we are in space, through what is called proprioception.

When the vestibular system is working well we know which direction we are moving in, how fast we are moving and whether we are speeding up or slowing down. Under normal conditions we are unaware of using it, but with illness or over-stimulation, for instance if we are travelling at sea or perhaps attempting to walk across a narrow beam, then we will become more conscious of our vestibular system at work and we become nauseous or feel threatened.

In order to get moving, your baby will have to come to terms with the input from her vestibular system, and the more input she has, the more it matures. Before your baby gets moving herself, she will rely on you to move her:

• She will find slow movements, like gentle rocking and swaying, soothing.
• Rapid movements, like jiggling, bouncing and swinging around will stimulate her.
• Carrying your baby in a sling is a great way to give her vestibular stimulation while allowing you to get on with other things.

Babies who are comforted by swaying and rocking are more visually alert than babies who are comforted through the other senses.

The vestibular system won't mature until your baby is around seven years of age, and continues to develop through puberty and beyond. Children seem very conscious of vestibular sensation – babies love being carried and rocked, children love going on roundabouts and swings. So don't worry if you seem to spend time carrying and jiggling your baby – you are helping her vestibular system develop, which is important not only for walking and general movement but for general intelligence. Children with learning difficulties such as Dyslexia, Dyspraxia, Attention Deficit, language impairment and/or emotional problems often have vestibular deficits; while adults who suffer from anxiety, agoraphobia and panic disorders are sometimes found to have problems with their vestibular systems.

While at first glance this might seem surprising, if you think about it, our vestibular system supplies our brains with a sense of direction, and many higher cognitive skills such as reading and writing require directional awareness (for example, the difference between 'saw' versus 'was', 'on' versus 'no'; telling the time involves being aware of up and down, left and right). Children who continue to reverse letters, numbers and words after age eight are often found to have an immature sense of balance.

In one study, researchers compared babies who had regular sessions of vestibular stimulation, being swung in different positions, with babies who did not receive this extra treatment, and found that the babies with the extra stimulation were more advanced in motor skills like sitting, crawling, standing and walking.

Movement and your baby's brain

There are at least three parts of the brain involved in movement, all of which interact with each other, but have slightly different functions. These are the cerebellum, the basal ganglia and the motor cortex.

- The **cerebellum** – a cauliflower shaped structure which sits above where the spinal cord merges with the rest of the brain – is like the autopilot of the brain. The cerebellum runs skills that have been acquired through practice and no longer need conscious control, like playing the piano or touch-typing. The vestibular system feeds into this structure and thus damage to the cerebellum results in poor co-ordination and clumsiness or ataxia.
- The **basal ganglia** lie below the cortex and span virtually the entire length of the brain. Damage to these result in movement disorders like Parkinson's disease and Huntington's chorea, cerebral palsy, stuttering and ADHD.
- The **motor cortex** sits over the brain like a hair band. It is responsible for our conscious actions, and is unique to us human beings. Any new action is probably controlled by the motor cortex, but once repeated often enough to become remembered, it is then controlled by the cerebellum.

The movements your baby makes at first are mostly under the control of the first two, more primitive regions of the brain. Some of these initial movements include reflex actions, such as the Moro or startle reflex, which emerges at 9 to 12 weeks after conception and is designed to respond to any unexpected event, particularly loss of head support. Your baby needs to outgrow her reflex actions before she can really master complicated, consciously thoughtout movements.

Moro reflex

If you lower your baby's head below the level of her spine, her arms and legs will fly open, there will be a sharp intake of breath and she will freeze in that position for a fraction of a second before bringing her arms and legs back across the body, usually with a strong cry of protest! This reflex helps your baby take her first breath, it usually fades by two months, and should be gone by four months. It has been suggested that if this reflex persists beyond four to six months, the baby is more sensitive and reactive, and may develop impulsive behaviour.

How your baby learns to use her hands

Holding on to something seems relatively simple, doesn't it? But in fact there is a long chain of events that the baby has to master before she can begin to use her hands competently.

Palmar Grasp reflex

In order to start manipulating objects with her hands, your baby is going to have to lose the Palmar Grasp reflex, which appears at birth and is fairly persistent until about the age of five to six months. Whenever an object is placed in her hand and touches her palm, she will grasp it. The grip is incredibly strong, but unpredictable, so she may either suddenly release whatever she is holding, or she might not be able to let go of it at all. That's why you should never try to lift your baby up with her holding on! In order to really interact with objects she is going to have to be able to let go at will; which is when the fun game of dropping toys over and over again can start.

Apart from losing the Palmar Grasp reflex, your baby has also got to co-ordinate her reaching behaviour; she's got to be able to sustain concentration or attention long enough to see an object, then reach for it adjusting her arm movements en route, touch the object and then open and close her hand on it. All this is more complicated than it might look; for a start your baby does not even realize for quite some time that her hands are attached to her and can be useful tools.

Reaching

Some psychologists have suggested that babies are capable of reaching behaviour at a very early age, others think it takes much longer. Whatever the case, the first obstacles are, ironically enough, her own hands.

What happens is that she spots an object, her arm starts to extend towards it, but halfway there she catches sight of her own hand. This is such an interesting sight that she stops reaching and stares at her hand instead. After a while she catches sight of the object again, starts to reach again, and then of course her hand distracts her again. This can go on for quite some time, with your baby alternating between being fascinated by the object and riveted by what her hand is doing. If her hand ever does make it on target, there is no guarantee that she will then manage the complex series of tasks involved in grasping that object. Instead you may well see your baby spending several days being completely obsessed by her hands. At this stage she just cannot cope with paying attention to two things; hand *and* object.

In some ways this doesn't matter as for quite a while she will be thoroughly entertained by the possibilities her hands present. She can grasp one hand with the other, bring both to her mouth, pull and push them apart and so on. At first she only uses them when they happen to pass in front of her eyes, but there is a magical moment when she realizes that they are attached to her own body (around five months of age) and can be brought into use whenever she needs them.

- In the first few weeks try putting something like a rattle in her hand, and see if she notices that when she moves her arm, it makes a noise. It will need to be fairly light for her to handle it. Alternatively you could strap a wrist rattle on and see what happens.
- Once she is really playing with her hands then she will enjoy rattles more.
- As she starts putting her hands in her mouth, then be aware that most things from now on will be explored in a similar way, so make sure everything is clean and not too small so that she might choke.
- If she has a dummy, then save it for sleepy times only as otherwise she will miss out on the chance to explore objects with her mouth.

Fine finger control

From six months onwards your baby will want to explore and handle lots of different objects. She'll no longer be satisfied with playing with her hands, and once she has explored the properties of one object she will want to move onto another. For the next few months she will refine her grasping and holding technique, from a general all fingers shut on one object through to holding two objects at once, one in each hand, then being able to separately control her fingers until she is able to point with one finger, and grasp very small things between finger and thumb. By one year of age she will have refined it so far that she can pick up a single raisin between thumb and forefinger.

- Give her a variety of objects to hold: toy bricks, wooden spoons, crinkly paper, bunches of keys, plastic cups and fluffy teddies. There is no need to invest in hundreds of toys; you will have plenty of things around the house that will provide her with hours of entertainment. Just make sure they are big enough not to choke on.
- Let her practise fine finger control on small pieces of food like cubes of cheese or soft bread, raisins and so on.
- Don't splash out on big toys at this stage as she won't be able to use them properly.

Case study

Jessica and Peter's baby Alexandra gets very frustrated with the limitations of her own body, and so they've always tried to help her. At first they helped by propping her up between their legs or surrounding her with cushions, but now they are convinced that Alexandra is ready to walk. She does not seem interested in crawling and hates being on her tummy, but continually tries to pull herself upwards. They are wondering whether it's time to buy a baby walker.

Some babies, particularly if they are very social and like lots of face-to-face interaction, don't really show much interest in crawling, and prefer to wait until they are able to walk. It doesn't mean they can't crawl, simply that they don't really bother. Babies also attempt to pull themselves upright and to stand for some time before they are capable of walking. It is a mistake to try to accelerate your baby's walking as the risk of accidents is then much higher. Baby walkers have been found to be the cause of many accidents in the home and so Jessica and Peter should really avoid this temptation. It would be far better if they arranged their furniture so Alexandra could practise 'cruising' from place to place. Although she might seem frustrated with her progress, the best her parents can do is be sympathetic!

Summary of this chapter

- Your baby's muscle control develops top to toe.
- As far as motor development goes, there is no race, and being advanced physically does not help your baby mentally.
- The vestibular system is important in motion and co-ordination, and deficits in the vestibular system can be linked to developmental disorders.
- Your baby needs to learn to let go before she can learn to grab hold!

What this means for you and your baby

You can have a lot of fun tracking your baby's development, but it is unlikely that you can advance your baby's progress any faster than she is going already. Try to give your baby lots of opportunities to be in different positions every day, and spend time carrying her around as this will improve her vestibular system and help her sense of balance.

There is no need to buy lots of different toys as most household objects, provided they are clean and safe, can give hours of amusement.

03 welcome to the world – the first six weeks

In this chapter you will learn:
- what your newborn baby can do
- how your newborn baby sees the world
- how to use this information to stimulate or calm your baby.

A newborn human baby is one of the most helpless beings on the planet, yet he arrives in the world with nine months of experience and many inborn skills.

While your baby may appear to have little control over his limbs, in fact he is already capable of some amazing feats, all of which are essential tools for survival.

Arriving on planet earth – being born

For nine months your baby has been growing in a protected environment: oxygen and food continually flowing into his body, his temperature kept stable by the warm water surrounding him, he was completely comfortable. His main challenge if you like was the input through his ears: he could hear continual noise in the womb; a rhythmic heartbeat, a whoosh of blood and digestion, and above all this, the sounds from the outside world, getting louder and more distinct as the day approached for him to be born.

As he goes through the process of birth, his mother's hormones and his own stress hormones combine so that as he is born he is hyperaware and alert, able to cope with this transition from one world to the next, and also interested in finding out where he is and who is there.

Meanwhile his mother too is 'hormonally charged' – ready to make contact with this new person. Most mothers unconsciously stimulate their babies after birth in various ways; stroking them, touching, making eye contact while automatically holding their babies so they are at the right distance to see, cuddling and talking to them.

Many of the painkillers that you might take during labour will affect your baby, making him less alert than he might otherwise be, and babies who are born by elective caesarean section do not have this build up of hormones to make the transition to this world easier. If you can attend NCT antenatal classes, the teacher there will go into some detail about your options for pain relief in labour, and this is time well spent as you will be far more aware of the implications of these choices on your newborn baby.

What your newborn baby can do

Scientists in Norway videoed babies who were delivered onto their mothers' stomachs, and found to their astonishment that if left to their own devices, the babies used their limbs in a slow but co-ordinated way to crawl up until they reached the breast, where they then latched on and fed, unaided. This incredible achievement, which combines the stepping, rooting and suckling reflexes, actually took over an hour, but it shows that newborn babies can do quite a lot, it just takes them longer to do so.

Your baby is born with several other reflexes, which involve complicated, co-ordinated body movements. The Palmar Grasp reflex means that he will tightly grasp things that are put in his hand, although it won't be until about four months that he deliberately reaches out, grasps an object and then, probably, puts it in his mouth. If he is startled by a loud noise or feels the sensation of falling, the Moro reflex makes him throw his head back, extend his arms, legs and fingers, and then bring them all together as if grasping. A sensible strategy if falling out of a tree, but with his heavy limbs he would not be able to hang on for long.

So it is not that your baby is physically incapable, it is just that his muscles are not yet strong enough to support his heavy body, and will need several months of use to build them up. You can see how well he can do things when he doesn't have this weight to contend with – look at him extending and flexing his fingers and toes, feel his strong and sustained grip on your finger. He can also co-ordinate and control the hundreds of muscles in his face when he cries, opens his eyes, or smiles.

What your newborn baby can sense

Your baby will have to work out what is around him, interpreting and understanding various sensations, and initially this is a pretty big task.

You probably think of yourself as having only five sense organs registering five different types of input, namely that your eyes, ears, skin, mouth and nose tells you what you see, hear, feel, taste or smell. In fact we can be aware of up to ten different types of sensations, using at least six different sensory organs (if we include the vestibular system in the inner ear) and of course most of this will be new to your baby when he is born.

For instance, our internal organs give us information about how comfortable we are; whether we are hungry or thirsty, whether we need to eliminate waste – these feelings are called interoception; for a newborn baby this is entirely new, as previously the placenta did all this for him.

Feeling overloaded

As adults we are usually unaware of a lot of this input, but think for a minute about the newborn baby, experiencing all of this and having to make sense of everything, most of it for the first time. He can easily become overloaded when coming to terms with what's going on in his tummy at the same time as trying to figure out what that noise is, and where he is, and there is a smell of milk – where is it? As adults we can filter a lot of it out and choose what to pay attention to, but it's hard work for babies. No wonder they can quickly become over-stimulated and fall asleep!

How your baby's sense of smell and taste works

Interestingly, foetuses can smell; scents carry in the amniotic fluid, and your baby's sense of smell develops around 28 weeks gestation. Throughout the third trimester, he can smell everything his mother can, as the placenta becomes more permeable, allowing in molecules from the outside world. This is probably why a newborn baby can identify his mother after birth; newborn baby girls respond to the smell of their own amniotic fluid, and apparently prefer to feed from a breast moistened with amniotic fluid, though there is no obligation to test this! (Newborn baby boys don't appear to manage this; a possible reason is that testosterone decreases the sense of smell.)

During pregnancy the mother's own smell changes so that it is a mixture of her own and her baby's, and this helps her to identify her own baby very soon after birth. In an experiment, mothers of one-day-old babies were asked to choose between three t-shirts, one worn by their own baby and the other two worn by other newborn babies, and even mothers who had spent as little as ten minutes with their own babies could correctly identify their baby's t-shirt. (See also Chapter 11 for fathers' responses to babies' smells.)

Unwashed babies are more successful at bringing their hand to their mouth to self-comfort in the first hour after birth than babies who have been washed, suggesting that they use smell to locate a source of comfort. Within six days your baby will recognize the smell of his own mother's milk and will turn his head towards it. Bottle-fed babies too can learn their parents' smell as long as they have plenty of close contact, so if you are bottle-feeding your baby, do make sure he has plenty of time being held 'skin to skin', i.e. with his naked body tucked inside your clothes.

Older babies are thought to scent mark their parents with their saliva – through breastfeeding and, later, through tears and general drool! This is how attachment objects (cuddlies) become important, and why children get so upset if a favourite teddy is washed. Children as young as three years can also identify their own siblings through the t-shirt sniffing experiment.

Taste is closely linked to smell, and works through chemical receptors on the tongue which are sensitive to salty, sour, bitter and sweet taste respectively, though in babies, the salty receptors are not well developed, and they particularly love sweet tastes. Smell works in a similar way in that molecules are chemically perceived by receptors in the nose. These go directly to emotion centres in the brain among other places, which explains why smells evoke such strong emotions and memories.

- Your baby's sense of smell is much stronger than yours, and he will be getting to know you in the early weeks through his sense of smell among other things, so try to avoid really strong perfumes, deodorants or washing powder, and be aware that some household smells may be quite over-powering for him.
- Some smells will also be soothing – the smell of his mother and father, the smell of his mother's breast milk, and so he may well be comforted by lying near an unwashed t-shirt or having a used breast pad nearby.
- If you like aromatherapy oils, then you can use these very diluted (so you can barely smell them) in your baby's room, but don't use them in massage; they will be too strong. Instead, put a few drops of calming oil on a cloth near his cot.

Why touch is important for your baby

Our skin can sense three different types of input: temperature, pain and pressure. Once our sense of touch is mature we can work out where we've been touched, how hard and even what we are touching. Our sense of touch is closely linked to our emotions, and touch is incredibly important for your baby. It is one of the most advanced senses at birth, and premature babies born as early as 25 weeks gestation are aware of being touched. While in the womb, touch seems to be the earliest sensation your baby will be aware of. Touch develops from head to toe, so the mouth is the first region to become sensitive, which is why young babies and children put everything in their mouths. However, although your baby can feel you touching him pretty well, he needs lots of touching experience to develop properly.

Your baby's brain will eventually contain a map of his body in his brain – the somatosensory region of the cerebral cortex – with large sections devoted to things like his fingertips, lips and tongue and relatively small areas devoted to legs and arms, so that these parts of the body are more sensitive to touch than others, and we can use them effectively. Although your baby's brain is genetically primed to develop this somatosensory map, it is also flexible, so for instance if your baby was born without fingers, that part of the map would not develop, and for the map to develop normally, your baby will need plenty of touching experience, and at this stage, that means being cuddled.

- As was true for smell, so too can your baby be comforted or stimulated through touch.
- Soothing touch might be massage, stroking, general cuddling.
- Stimulating touch includes tickling, gentle touches to his face, feet and hands.
- Your baby can sense temperature and although he can't throw off clothing or bedding to cool down, he can do other things. When he is cool he will move around more and when he is warm he will lie as if he is 'sunbathing' with his arms and legs flung out to the side. You can use these signs to work out if your baby is too hot or too cold without having to disturb him.
- Encourage all members of your family to cuddle your baby, and to get used to holding and handling your baby – all these experiences will be helpful for him as well as giving you a break!

What your baby can hear

Sound is carried on airwaves, caught by the folds of the outer ear and channelled into and registered by receptors inside the ear. In learning to hear, babies have to learn to identify where sounds comes from and then attach a meaning to each sound.

Babies start learning about their world while in the womb, and sound is the medium which connects them to the outside world. Lower frequencies actually carry better in the womb than higher, so father's voice travels well, though mother's is clearest as it's coming directly through her body.

Your baby will start responding to sounds from as early as 20 weeks gestation, and will be actively processing this auditory input, distinguishing between music, language and other sounds. Newborn babies are interested in complex sounds (whereas they prefer simple visual input), and the reason hearing is so important is that it gives your baby a head start in tuning into the language he will speak.

At birth your baby will move his body in synchrony with human speech, and after two days, he will prefer to listen to his mother's native language than to a foreign language.

In one experiment, women who were pregnant were asked to read the Dr Suess' story *The Cat in the Hat* aloud twice a day during the last six weeks of their pregnancy. Shortly after birth their babies were tested to see if they preferred hearing *The Cat in the Hat* or another story – *The king, the mice and the cheese* – and they preferred *The Cat in the Hat,* even when read by an unfamiliar voice. Another researcher found that newborn babies stopped crying when they heard the themes from soaps that their mothers had watched during pregnancy.

Babies can tell the difference between their mother's voice and another female voice two hours after they are born, which means that they were learning to recognize her voice in utero.

Fascinating fact
Babies like their mothers' voices distorted!

Interestingly, your baby hears his mother's voice in utero distorted in the same way as she hears her own voice, as the sound is travelling through her body and not through the sound waves as we might hear other people's voices. And in fact, newborn babies do initially prefer the sound of their mother's voice distorted as if it were heard in utero.

- Your baby will find certain sounds soothing, particularly familiar sounds like his mother's and father's voices, songs and music that he has heard before.
- You might like to set up positive associations for your baby before he is born: play your favourite music to him during pregnancy, and you will find that it calms him after birth.
- Sing gently to your newborn baby, or hum with your head pressed next to his head when rocking him, and see how he reacts.
- Some babies who initially find it difficult to calm down and go to sleep, may be able to drift off with music playing, others like to have a recording of their parents' conversations. You could also try putting your baby monitor in reverse so he can hear you rather than you hearing him.
- Many babies find sounds which remind them of the womb very comforting, so any white noise such as tumble driers, vacuum cleaners, hairdryers or car engines can work. You can buy special womb noise tapes, or make your own by recording your baby's favourite white noise!

What can babies see?

While sight is probably our most important sense as adults, and indeed our brains have larger areas devoted to vision than to all the other senses combined, for babies it is the least well developed at birth, probably because it has not been stimulated in the womb. Newborn babies cannot see as well as adults; they lack the ability to see detail, they cannot easily track moving objects with their eyes but do this fairly jerkily, and they are not good at scanning objects (casting their eyes over the inside of an object). They cannot detect many colours; at birth they can tell the difference between red and white, but not between white and other colours.

For the first three months of life your baby can focus on things about 22 cms or 9 inches away – the best distance for seeing his mother's face when feeding, and for focusing on his own body, particularly his hands. He is sensitive to light – he will turn towards a diffuse light, but shut his eyes against a bright light. He can track moving objects, particularly if they are face-like.

In fact, imagine looking at the world through frosted glass; that is how it is for your newborn baby. This poor vision is useful at this age though, as probably going from seeing nothing to seeing everything would probably be a terrible shock, so rather than being overwhelmed by detail, they are primed to take notice of certain things, as we shall see later on. Being able to focus on things close up not only means that they can concentrate on human faces, but also that they can start co-ordinating eye and hand movements.

- There is not much point in worrying about your baby's visual environment in the early weeks. It will not calm your baby to put him in normal visual range because he will not be able to see you.
- When you want your baby to see you, hold him in your arms; this is the perfect focusing distance for him.
- At this stage, concentrate on the other senses for stimulating or calming your baby.

What you can do to settle your baby

The first six weeks of life for your baby are going to involve coming to terms with this new world, in particular establishing new patterns; distinguishing day and night, gradually developing a cycle of sleep and wakefulness. In all of this your help will be invaluable.

Does a newborn baby need to sleep a lot?

All babies need to sleep a lot, partly to rest from the physical and mental stimulation of being alive, but also to process all the new information they constantly receive. When your baby is over-stimulated he will probably fall asleep as a coping strategy. He won't have any problem sleeping through noise after nine months of din in the uterus, and may well prefer noise; just look at the number of babies you see fast asleep in the noisiest of places! From your point of view it is better that he is used to sleeping through noise anyway as it will give you more flexibility; you won't need to tiptoe around when he has gone to bed, and you can go out to noisy places knowing that he won't miss his naps.

Initially your baby will drift between sleeping and waking randomly and erratically. It may even be difficult to tell when he is asleep or awake. As you probably don't want a baby who dozes off and on day and night, you will need gradually, over the first few months, to teach him about sleeping and waking. It is best to try and establish the difference between night and day, so perhaps you might develop a soothing bedtime routine to indicate the end of the day, and when he wakes during the night, be quiet and calm, soothe and feed him back to sleep.

An example of a soothing bedtime routine might be:

- Warm bath
- Different night clothes
- Sing a lullaby
- Gentle massage
- Warm milk feed
- Tuck up in bed with a ritual phrase, e.g. nightie night, sleep tight.

It doesn't exactly matter what you do, as long as the elements of the routine are calming and not stimulating, and as long as you do the same things every day. It will take some time, but eventually the routine in itself will make your baby sleepy.

During the day, your baby will need a fair amount of sleep, but after the first couple of weeks, you may wish to establish wakeful periods, by making these lively and stimulating, holding your baby upright to keep him awake. By six weeks he will have re-established his diurnal rhythms, should need slightly less daytime sleep, and playtimes will get longer and more interesting.

Crying – the last ditch communication

Everyone hears a crying baby. We can screen out phones, traffic noise, conversations, but only an adult who is mentally disturbed can totally ignore a baby in distress. You will quickly tune into your own baby's sounds; after only three nights most mothers on hospital wards wake immediately for their own baby's cry.

It will take longer to learn what his different cries mean. Pain is quite distinctive with breath holding in the middle. Hunger, tiredness and boredom are easily confused, however.

Rather than wait for your baby to cry and then have to do damage limitation, it is worth trying to anticipate that state and intervene before your baby is upset. It can help to think about your baby moving through a cycle of alertness in these first few weeks, thus:

Deeply asleep – dozing – quiet alert – active alert – fussing – crying.

Quiet alert is when a baby is wide-eyed and interested, but calm and still. Your baby is most likely to be in this phase when he is being held or carried. Active alert is when your baby is not only wide-awake, but also moving around a lot, wriggly or kicking.

What you can do is when your baby is in active alert stage, watch for signs of him entering the fussy state, the downwards spiral to crying, and try to calm down the stimulation before he gets worked up and harder to soothe.

Cues might be: squirming, arching his back, yawning, turning away from you, frowning grimacing or possetting (bringing up milk).

It will take you time to work out which strategies work in calming him down. Not all strategies will work all the time, and anyway it is best to try one at a time to avoid overloading him, but anything that is a reminder of that womb-like state will help.

- Swaddle your baby if he startles easily.
- Cover your baby with a blanket if he dislikes nappy changing.
- Help him find his thumb or fist to suck on if he is a sucky baby.
- Some babies like watching mobiles or other moving patterns especially if they involve a lot of contrast and are close enough to catch his eye.
- Others prefer to listen to lullabies or white noise like hairdryers or tumble driers.
- Rocking in a horizontal position can help if your baby is tired.
- Rocking more intermittently in an upright position might work for your baby when he is wide-awake and distressed.
- Sometimes babies need to go into a dark room if they find the light too much.

At six weeks most babies go through a grizzly patch which can be hard, and babies who cry a lot, particularly in the evening, are referred to as having colic, though all babies do fuss at this stage. One theory is that baby's brain is 'rewiring', getting ready for the next developmental stage.

Colic

Scientists are still trying to figure out why some babies cry more than others, though we think colic is simply one end of a spectrum of normal behaviour. There is no evidence that colic is anything to do with how you parent your baby, though responding to his cries for help is important; leaving babies to cry it out actually makes them cry *more* when they are older and feel more insecure, and you can find out why in Chapter 09.

About 10–15 per cent of excessive crying is a reaction to cows' milk protein, either in formula milk, or through dairy products in a breastfeeding mother's diet. Other babies find it hard to cope with the shift towards the day/night cycle and again others are particularly sensitive and find it hard to manage any changes or different stimulation.

All colicky babies are harder to settle once they become unsettled, and most go straight from active alert to crying without giving you a chance to intervene at the fussy stage.

All you can do is to try as many strategies as you can, keep trying them, and get other people to help, either in soothing your baby or in supporting you in your attempts.

Massage

Massaging your baby can be stimulating, soothing, and great fun for both of you. Your health visitor may run classes herself or know of local classes, but you can have a go with these simple strokes. You don't need to use any oils, but if you want to then stick to very simple vegetable-based oils.

- Arms – stroke both arms simultaneously from the top of your baby's shoulders down to his hands. Pause, and then repeat by letting go one side at a time and moving your hand back to his shoulder to start again.
- Indian milking – place both your hands near the top of one arm then move one hand at a time down the arm to the wrist in a milking motion. Always leave one hand in contact. Do the same action on his legs
- Hands – press your thumbs into his palms, roll and squeeze his fingers from the base to the tips. Do the same for his feet.
- Tummy – move your hand in a clockwise direction around his tummy, which is the direction of intestines, using gentle pressure.
- Place your hands under his arms next to his ribcage, slide one hand down his side to the groin closely followed on the other side by the other hand; as the first hand reaches his groin, lift it and place it back under the ribs to start again, keeping the other hand in contact. Do the same on his back: starting at his shoulders, swoop your hands slowly down to his bottom.

Interacting with your newborn baby

Your relationship with him will be his first and most important, and will set him up for life as a social being.

Your baby is born ready to be sociable. He is attracted to listen to patterned sounds rather than monotones, especially those in the same frequency as the human voice. He is interested in tracking moving visual stimuli with lots of contour information, particularly if similar to the human face, and his focusing distance is about right for close interaction. His life depends on being close, not only to see you but to keep warm and safe, and his whole being is designed to make you want to keep him close, whether it is that appealing round forehead and chubby limbs, or the last resort crying which no one can ignore.

He will want to communicate non-verbally with you as soon as he is born. At first he will attempt to imitate you. Try sticking your tongue out at him. Slowly, after about 30 seconds, he should copy. Talk to your baby, and look out for, and answer all his 'responses'. For example, he might open his mouth wide while looking at you, making an obvious effort for a number of seconds. Sometimes you see his limbs moving – arms rising, fingers opening and pointing – for him this is 'conversation'.

Your baby will tire quickly at this stage, so don't expect too much and make the most of those alert moments to communicate with him.

In a few weeks he will want you to imitate him, and he will love it if you copy his expressions. This you will probably do intuitively, using your whole face and voice to 'mirror' what he is doing, giving your baby clear and enriched feedback of his own action. This mirroring helps your baby establish a sense of self, and you can find out more about this in Chapter 14.

Timing is an important learning process; not too slow and not too quick; but don't worry about this because mismatches are part of learning to communicate. At times your baby will become highly aroused and excited during these conversations and may get overloaded quickly, breaking off eye contact or frowning or grimacing. Little and often will work best.

Babies only a few weeks old wave their arms in time to speech, much as we adults gesture while we speak, and what they are doing is practising the rhythm of speech. As your baby gets older, he will start gesturing at you, trying to talk. He will move his mouth around, and wave his arms excitedly when he sees you. He wriggles with glee when he knows it is time for a feed or a bath. When you talk, he will tune his movements in to the rhythm of your voice, and without knowing it, you will tune into his pattern.

Most baby mammals suck mechanically and steadily at the breast, however your baby will tend to suckle, pause, suckle, pause. How long he pauses for will depend on how you respond. If you do nothing, he won't pause for long; however if you chat to him or jiggle him, he will pause for longer, until you finish, and then start suckling again. He is politely waiting for you to take your turn. Psychologists refer to this as 'proto-conversation'; the first signs of your baby 'chatting' with you.

- Your newborn baby prefers human speech to any other similar sounds. When he is older and learning to talk, he will try to imitate human sounds rather than inanimate noises such as the telephone ringing.
- A baby can work out where a sound is coming from, ten minutes after he is born. Before the end of his first week, he will know your voice.

Early communication: that first smile

Your baby is born to smile. We know this because blind babies also smile, so it's not just copying. His earliest, 'reflex' smile may happen in the first few days, usually when he is dropping off to sleep, or hears your voice. By four to six weeks you will see a different, more definite smile. Your baby is pretty unselective at this age, he will smile at most things, including a circle with dots on it.

Developmental checks in the first six weeks

Apgar scores

The first developmental check your baby will encounter is the Apgar score, a rating done by your midwife immediately after birth, and again at five minutes after birth. A score of 7–10 is healthy, 4–6 is somewhat depressed, and below 4 is cause for concern, particularly at five minutes.

Score			
	0	1	2
Skin tone	Blue-grey, pale all over	Normal except for extremities	Normal over entire body
Heart rate	Absent	Slow (less than 100 beats per minute)	Over 100
Response to stimulation	No response	Grimace	Crying
Muscle tone	Flaccid	Some flexing in extremities	Active movement
Breathing	Absent	Slow, irregular	Good, crying

Heel-prick test

At around day six your baby will be given some blood tests to screen for several rare disorders including cystic fibrosis, phenylketonuria (PKU), low thyroid functioning and blood problems. He will be given a prick in the heel to collect a sample of blood.

Your baby's growth

You will be given a Child Health Record booklet which includes records of immunizations, routine health and developmental checks. It also contains centile charts on which to plot your baby's growth. There are different charts for boys and girls, but the principles are the same. Birth weight is recorded and plotted on the chart at EDD (Expected Delivery Date), even if your baby was late. If premature, the first plot will be before EDD.

The first plot will fall on a certain 'centile', or percentage line. For instance, if your baby is on the 2nd centile, it means only 2 per cent of newborn babies weigh the same or less than your baby, the 50th centile means your baby's weight is average, while 98th means 98 per cent of newborns weigh less than yours.

Every time your baby is weighed, the measurement is plotted on the chart. He's expected to gain weight at around the same rate as other babies and therefore his weight gain should roughly remain on the same centile line.

The book contains similar charts for head circumference (or brain growth) and body length, which should also be recorded regularly.

Newborn babies usually lose weight at first – up to 7 per cent is considered normal, due mostly to passing a first bowel motion of meconium, a black sticky tar-like substance which protected the gut in utero. Most babies regain their birth weight within two to three weeks, although premature babies can take longer, as will babies who lose more than 7 per cent initially. If you had analgesics late in labour, your baby may be sleepy for several days and unwilling to feed. Jaundiced babies will also be sleepy and need encouragement to feed.

What it means if your baby is not following the charts

Centile charts represent an average British baby, who statistically speaking was born at full term, weaned onto solids early and who was bottle-fed (though breast-fed charts are now becoming available). If your baby is breast-fed, was premature or 'small for dates', comes from a family of tall or short people, the charts are less likely to be accurate.

Gains on the charts are quite small – an ounce or two here or there, and it is easy to get such minute amounts wrong. If your baby just had an enormous poo before weighing, this could make him lose an ounce, for instance. Scales vary, so check whether your health visitor is using the same scales each time.

Has your baby actually lost weight, or is he just not gaining the amount expected? A baby who has been ill, even if only a bit snuffly, may well have used his energy fighting bugs rather than gaining weight. It is also important to take into account how much weight your baby lost in his first few days, and measure any gains from that low point.

It is equally important to consider whether:

• your baby seems content and alert – does he interact with you?
• his skin is soft and moist, and if pinched or pressed it should return to normal immediately
• his eyes are bright and clear
• he has several really wet nappies a day (five disposables, six to eight washables)
• frequent (two or more per day) bowel moments if under six weeks, yellow and sweet smelling if breast-fed

- his cry is generally strong and insistent which stops when you attend to him. An irritable or fretful baby is not necessarily underfed, but is letting you know he needs you.

The above are all good signs. You need to worry if:

- his fontanelle is sunken
- wet nappies are few and far between, or smell strongly of urine which may be dark
- your baby's crying is prolonged, whiny and miserable, or
- your baby seems very placid, and rarely cries.

For most babies and young children, the occasional dip on the charts will not matter. However, if your baby is consistently slower than expected overall, you may need to seek help. Talk to your health visitor or GP and if you are still not sure, ask to be referred to a paediatrician. Your baby will be monitored and may simply be referred to as 'slow to gain weight'. 'Failure to thrive' is more serious and needs medical attention. If you are breastfeeding you may like to seek help from a breastfeeding counsellor. Avoid using dummies or other soothers for a while, and if your baby is placid and sleeps a lot, you may well need to wake him to remind him to feed.

Support for you

At this stage, it is going to be quite hard to get out of the house and do things, but try to meet up with other parents for support and help. The National Childbirth Trust runs Bumps and Babes groups; these are for pregnant women and parents with new babies to meet up for mutual support (see the Taking it Further section for contact details). They also organize post-natal support groups in your area, putting you in touch with other parents of babies the same age. From these groups might develop a babysitting circle which is tremendously helpful when you want to start going out together as a couple again (and see Chapter 11 for just why this is important).

Your health visitor should be a good source of support at this stage, and she may also be able to tell you about any local support groups such as breastfeeding support groups if you are breastfeeding; you don't have to have problems to attend these, it can be useful just to meet other women for a natter. The health visitor may also organize or know of local baby massage classes. These are worth going to, not only for meeting up with other people in the same situation, but also as a good way of learning about interacting with your baby.

> **Case study**
>
> *Maggie and Jim are really struggling with Connor, who is now six weeks old and seems to have colic. He cries inconsolably in the evenings, and during the day he is often unsettled and starts to cry very easily. They are worried about what they should do. Is this normal? They are doing their best to comfort Connor, but Jim's mother is suggesting that there is no harm in leaving him to cry on his own so they can get some peace.*
>
> It sounds as if Connor is a sensitive baby, and he may continue to be like this for some time to come. It is hard work, but if Maggie and Jim keep responding to him with care and attention, he will eventually settle, and be a far happier baby than he would be if they ignored his distress.
>
> It is probably sensible if they take turns to comfort Connor so they can each have a break, and perhaps get other friends and relatives to help. It also helps if they can stay calm themselves (not easy!) as Connor will pick up on their stress.

Fascinating newborn facts

- Researchers noticed when mothers first meet their newborn babies, they usually comment on their baby's appearance, and apparently often say how much he resembles the father. The researchers rather unkindly suggest this is perhaps to assure the men of paternity!
- Babies can't cry tears for at least three weeks, sometimes not until they reach four or five months of age. Tears contain stress hormones and so crying is a way of calming down after a fright. No other animals cry stress tears, so perhaps our tears are a signal, showing up against our skin. Mothers instinctively feel the need to clean up their children, so will cuddle them and dry their eyes.
- Babies only a few weeks old prefer to look at pretty women. This is because a pretty face is harmonious, representing an ideal or 'prototypical' face.
- Babies like being rocked and we instinctively rock them at heat-beat pace. When walking with a baby to soothe him, we slow our pace to this same rate.

- The average boy weighs 7 lbs 8 oz (3.4 kg) at birth, but this can vary from 5¹/₂ to 10 lbs (2.5–4.5 kg). The heaviest ever recorded weighed 23 lbs 12 oz, born in 1879 in Canada.

- Your baby's weight depends mostly on your size, but also on your health and your partner's size.

- The length of a term baby is between 45 and 55 cms, (18–22 in), with the average somewhere in the middle.

- At birth, his tummy is the size of a walnut, and so it can't hold much. This is why he will feed little and often.

- Being able to hear is of course necessary for learning to speak, so it is not surprising that your baby is born with very sophisticated hearing. Not only will he recognize your voice, psychologists have found that two-day-old babies still knew their mothers from a tape recording of only one syllable.

- Psychologists in Arizona found that even newborn babies have an elementary grasp of maths and physics. They can tell the difference between one, two, three and more objects, and also can add up and take away. They may not have an abstract concept of numbers, but they know how many apples should remain, for instance, if one is taken away, and express surprise if it is wrong.

- Babies love to learn, and get immense satisfaction from solving problems. Newborn babies loved being able to switch a light off and on by turning their head, two-month-old babies giggled with delight when they found that they could make their cot mobile dance about.

04

your baby wakes up – six weeks to six months

In this chapter you will learn:

- how your baby develops control over her body to start manipulating objects
- that babies can express their feelings and understand emotions in others
- about the critical role you play in managing your baby's emotions
- how babies communicate at this stage.

For many parents, this is the stage when they feel that they fall in love with their babies for the first time – and no wonder! The first smile, the first laugh, the coos and babbles – babies of this age can be adorable.

Your baby's physical development

Although your baby will remain immobile at this stage of development, there are many amazing things she will accomplish, and it can be fascinating to watch and help her achieve all these feats.

Using her hands

Over this time period, the Palmar Grasp reflex fades to be replaced gradually by more deliberate interaction with objects.

In order for your baby to really start playing with objects and exploring the world around her, she is going to need to co-ordinate looking, reaching and grasping, and these behaviours will mature over this period. These skills will take time to consolidate, but the more practice she has the quicker she will manage, so your interventions can help.

In the early weeks your baby may play with objects if they are put in her hand; so she might well wave a rattle around and enjoy the noise it makes, but she is not able to play with something and look at it at the same time, thus her use of objects is fairly restricted.

At three months of age she will probably bring her hands together and look at them and also play with her fingers, but it will take her a few more months to be able to co-ordinate all these skills so she can look at something, reach out and grab objects within reach. Even when she does achieve this level of co-ordination, she will only hold things in a fist; fine finger control comes later, so she will still be limited in the range of objects she can examine.

- Spend some time each day with your baby sitting on your lap and hold various objects in front of her, close enough for her to see and grasp. Look to see if she makes an attempt to reach for these objects – it may take her a bit of time.
- Move the objects back and forward slowly in front of her to help practice visual tracking.
- Put a variety of objects into her hand and let her understand what they do: try rattles, soft toys, bells, crinkly paper.

- Tie a mobile over her cot and vary the objects that hang there – black and white circles are good, but try also pendants which catch the light, varied shapes, wind chimes and other objects. (Avoid over-stimulating your baby if you want her to sleep though.)

What is also maturing at this time is her understanding of objects (see Chapter 14). For most of this period, your baby will not understand that things she cannot see continue to exist. By six months though, she will begin to grasp this concept, and this may well be the time that that fascinating game starts: drop something and watch Mum and Dad retrieve it!

- If you don't mind handing the toy back time and time again, you will be letting her take control of the world by allowing her to make things happen. Tell yourself you are aiding her intellectual development!
- This tendency to drop everything can really backfire though, so it is worth tying everything onto prams or car seats when you are out of the house if you don't want to spend your days retracing steps to find precious teddies, etc.

Controlling her body

This period of time is exciting and frustrating, as your baby gradually gains control over her body, and by six months she may well be able to sit up for extended periods of time. Be aware of the frustrating time leading up to this when she wants to sit, but ends up sliding off to one side or the other. Variety seems to help:

- Have some time sitting propped up with cushions or in a baby nest.
- Then swap to a doorway bouncer.
- Afterwards have some time in a sling facing outwards.
- Try a few minutes lying on her back with her nappy off for a good kicking session.
- Don't forget tummy time too!
- Finish with time walking outside in a pram.

Getting to know each other's emotions

Even at birth, babies are capable of letting us know how they feel. Initially, babies just feel a sort of generalized positive or negative emotional state, but as adults respond to them, they begin to understand, refine and communicate these emotions. In a way, emotions are their first language. How well your baby can manage her emotional states will, however, depend on you.

Within a few weeks, mothers say that they can tell whether their babies are happy, interested, surprised, sad, fearful, angry or in pain. Of course context helps – if your baby has just had a nice experience it's safe to guess she is happy, but it does also seem true that babies can express different emotions through facial expressions and body language. The only emotions which are hard to tell apart are anger and pain; what you appear to see is just distress, but by six months it will become easier for you to tell these emotional states apart as well.

Babies know how we feel too. They can monitor our tone of voice, for instance, if you smiled at your baby while talking to her in a frightened tone of voice, or did the reverse – spoke in a happy voice with a scared expression on your face, you would probably find that your baby would get extremely agitated, not knowing which cues to respond to. You may also notice that even as early as ten weeks, if you appear happy or angry, your baby will also seem happy or angry.

What seems to happen is that throughout this stage your baby will look carefully at you to work out what you are feeling in order to know how to react; psychologists call this 'social referencing'. This is one of the reasons it's extremely hard to soothe a crying baby if you feel tense and upset yourself.

Later on, around seven or eight months when your baby develops 'fear of strangers' (see Chapter 09), she will look at you to see how you respond to the appearance of a stranger, and take her cues from you. If you seem relaxed, your baby will be less fearful.

How babies feel

Babies are not able to control their own emotions. Before their frontal cortex develops, which is the part of the brain that can rationalize things for us and which does not even begin to develop until well after birth (see Chapter 08), emotions feel far more primitive and immediate for your baby than they do for us as adults. What they experience are generalized feelings of distress or contentment but with little complexity.

If you want to get inside a baby's head, think of what it feels like when you get an unexpected fright and adrenaline surges through your system: you jump, your hair stands on end and your heart starts pounding. As your cortex kicks in and tells you, 'don't worry, it was just a balloon bursting', you can feel that rational part of your brain calming you down. But for the baby, until parents respond with calming actions, that flight or fright response remains activated. They can't rationalize themselves out of it. Having said that, unless the experience is really traumatic, they don't remember feeling upset once you calm them down, they can't linger on thinking about it, and have no way of recalling memories of bad times.

How adults calm babies

Watch an experienced mother pick up her crying baby and you will see a very effective strategy, and one that she probably uses without thinking, which is to calm her baby by mirroring her emotion and then leading her out of that state by example.

So as her baby cries, the mother matches the volume of that cry with words of comfort, in order to catch the baby's attention. Her face will mirror the baby's look of distress. Once the baby has noticed, the mother progressively calms her own voice down, relaxing her facial expression, until the two are calm together. This mirroring and exaggerating baby's emotional state and facial expressions, 'showing me my feelings', is called 'psychofeedback'.

You too can use this very effective technique:

- Hold your baby so she can see into your eyes.
- Speak calmly but loudly to her until you get her attention.
- Gentle swaying or jiggling will help get her attention and will also feel calming.
- Let her know that you understand how she feels.
- Once she is looking at you, lower your voice, start to widen your eyes and smile.

Why babies cry

Babies cannot manage their emotional states, but they have several qualities which make sure we want to help them. Firstly they look endearing and we want to pick them up and cuddle them. Those large round foreheads, tiny noses, big round eyes are deeply ingrained signals for all mammals which cartoonists exploit – next time you watch a cartoon, see how the artist exaggerates these baby signals to increase the 'awww...' factor.

Secondly, when they get emotionally out of kilter, they cry, and the baby's cry is an extremely powerful signal. They wail at a volume which is completely out of proportion to their body size. In fact if their crying were scaled up to adult proportions, the decibel level would be roughly that of a pneumatic drill!

Crying is such a powerful tool that parents quickly become motivated to avoid that noise, and to respond to their babies' signals before things escalate into crying. Within a short space of time, parents who take the time to tune into their babies, tend to start noticing the little signals that tell them their baby needs help before they start crying. Rooting tells them the baby needs feeding; grimacing, squirming, rubbing eyes and averting gaze tell them that the baby needs time out. Some babies posset when they become over-stimulated.

This early tuning in involves parents in spending time getting to know their babies, but is worth doing because babies whose parents respond to their needs quickly, will cry less as they get older.

Some signs that your baby needs time out
Remember not all babies will use all these signs, but if these become familiar to you as preceding a period of fussiness and crying, then use them as a signal that it's time for a break, time to wind down stimulation:

- Screwing up face, grimacing.
- Averting eyes, closing eyes.
- Posseting (bringing up small amounts of milk).
- Bringing thumb to mouth.
- Turning head away, twisting body.

Stress hormones in your baby

If you are emotionally aroused for long periods of time and unable to calm yourself down, you become stressed, and people under stress have higher levels of the hormone cortisol in their bloodstreams.

Human babies are born expecting to have stress managed for them and tend to have low levels of cortisol for the first few months as long as caring adults maintain their equilibrium through touch, stroking and feeding, but the baby's immature systems are also very unstable and reactive. If they are not helped, their cortisol levels can shoot up and they are not capable of bringing these down on their own.

Babies who are left to cry on their own tend to have high levels of cortisol in their bloodstream, and there is now evidence that too much cortisol early on can affect the developing brain so that babies who were left to 'cry it out' grow up to be adults who are less able to handle stress.

Sleep can reduce cortisol levels, which is why babies who are left to cry to sleep do eventually fall asleep. They simply have to shut down to recover from their raised cortisol levels. So the 'controlled crying' which is advocated in some sleep books – leaving your baby to cry himself to sleep does work, but at the cost of having a more stressed baby. Of course the baby will recover from this if it is a one-off event; the problem is when parents use it as a long-term strategy for 'helping' babies to sleep.

How do babies get stressed?

Some babies are more sensitive and need more soothing and calming than other babies. Some get stressed in the womb; a mother who has a stressful pregnancy or who smokes during pregnancy for instance, is likely to give birth to a stressed baby, but others seem to be sensitive without cause. If you have a very sensitive baby, as long as you continue to respond to her and attempt to soothe her, in time she will become a calm individual who will actually cry less than a baby whose parents were not as responsive.

Fascinating fact

Babies can sense how their mother feels even in the womb!

In one study, researchers asked pregnant women to wear headphones and listen to various types of music while they measured their babies' movements with ultrasound. The researchers found that most of the babies became more active when the music was on, especially if their mother was listening to music she liked.

What is fascinating here is that the babies could not hear the music; it was only audible to the mothers, so the babies were responding to their mothers' emotional responses to the music.

That is not to say that crying creates stress for a baby; crying is a healthy mechanism for alerting parents to a potentially dangerous situation. Stress is only unhealthy for a baby when it is unrelieved, when babies are left to cry without any interventions from parents.

Some babies will still cry a lot at this stage – colic is defined as peaking at six weeks and disappearing by three months, but you might still be in for some rough times, and some babies continue to be quite fractious. However it may become easier for you to understand what your baby wants, and in addition, your baby begins to understand what happens when she cries, so that by five months of age, your baby will cry more deliberately. Typically she cries, waits to hear if you are coming, and then cries again. Because you have responded in the past, she is able to wait for your response and she is now getting better at telling you want she needs. The main thing you can do at this stage is to always respond to your baby when she cries; learning about delayed gratification comes much later and will be easier for your baby to learn and accept later if her needs are responded to at this stage.

Your sociable baby

Early on, your baby enjoys making vowel sounds and gurgles. She is already practising the noises she later fine-tunes for speech. However, language is not just for naming things; language is for communication, and from day one, your baby will be participating in conversations.

By six weeks she will start to practise the lip and tongue movements she will need for speaking, and she may now start to coo in response to your voice. In a couple more weeks, babbling will start in earnest. Soon she will be wriggling and cooing to attract your attention, and will love 'looking' conversations, where you make faces at each other and copy expressions, as well as games like peekaboo which are also precursors to conversation.

Pre-speech develops rapidly over this period; by three months your baby chats when she hears your voice, and by six months she uses recognizable sounds and double syllables, like da-da-da or mam-mam-mam.

It is really worth getting involved in these 'conversations'; these are vital for your baby's social development and for helping her to learn to speak. See below for some singing games you can play with your baby.

Smiling

Your baby's ability to focus her eyes will improve rapidly over this period, and by six months she will be able to see what you can see. As she learns to focus and to perceive more detail, she needs more detail too, so for instance in the first six weeks of life she will smile at simple dots or angles which are slightly face like, by ten weeks she needs more detail but will still smile just at eyes alone, but by 12 weeks she needs all of your face, particularly preferring a wide mouth, and eventually by 30 weeks, she will smile at particular, known faces.

- During this time then, make sure you put things so your baby can see them properly; for instance in the first three months you will still need to move in close for her to focus (about 30 cm).

- Watch how her smiles become more discriminating over this period, so by six months she will reserve her big social smile just for you.

Although babies will smile at most things early on, by six weeks she smiles at human faces – a true social smile. From now on you will see different types of smiles for different situations. There is the pleased to see you smile that she reserves for her parents and other familiar people. Her whole face lights up, eyes twinkle and her shoulders rise with pleasure. There is the delighted smile that she uses when she has made something happen. Then there is the amused smile which turns into a laugh at about four months of age.

The first joke is always shared with another trusted adult. Often it comes for a tickle or a boo; your baby is almost scared but because it is beloved Mummy or Daddy who is doing the scaring, with a smile on their face, she knows it is safe. The sudden breath that would have been a cry comes out as a laugh. We believe that adult humour is often about fear too and originates from these earliest jokes.

The first time your baby laughs is truly special. Babies laugh at the same sorts of things we do – silly, unexpected or slightly startling but not threatening things can all provoke a giggle. Once you have provoked a laugh, you will want it to happen over and again!

Recognizing faces

Newborn babies prefer to look at patterned objects rather than plain ones, but they also prefer less complex patterns the younger they are because they cannot take in the detail at this age. The patterns they prefer most of all though, are those nearest to a face.

Human beings have long thought there is something special about eye contact. Staring deep into another person's eyes will start a strong emotional reaction, whether of love, anger or fear, it's impossible to be neutral, and pupil size is an important non-verbal signal for human beings. If someone is looking at you with enlarged pupils, it's a good sign that they find you attractive, but if their pupils contract to pinpoints it is probably time to leave! Interestingly too, babies' pupils dilate just after they are born as an added attraction.

Evolutionary psychologists have suggested that this attentiveness to eye contact is probably innate in human beings and evolved to be useful in the days when we hunted together and needed to communicate without sound.

We know that newborn babies can recognize their own mother's face within a few days, but how do they do that? In fact when mothers wear scarves over their hair so that only the internal features of their faces are visible, newborn babies can't tell them apart from fairly similar looking women, although they would be able to do this without the scarves. So initially your baby relies on just the external boundaries of your face to recognize you; don't be surprised if she gives you a blank stare if you change your hair or wear a hat! Nevertheless we know that newborn babies also recognize facial expressions and can therefore respond to internal features, but only when they are moving.

Fascinating fact
Obligatory looking – help, I'm stuck!

Babies between one and two months can sometimes be seen staring at something for ages, and then seeming to get distressed. What happens is that they actually get stuck looking at something; psychologists call this obligatory looking. This happens because their visual cortex is maturing and starts to draw their eyes away from the edge of their visual field, but sometimes this overpowers them. The result is distress, but also sometimes it means long bouts of staring at you, and this is often the stage at which parents really feel they have 'fallen in love' with their baby.

Interacting with your baby

Babies respond to all voices from birth, but are particularly tuned to high-pitched voices (like their mother's). You must, therefore, talk all the time to your baby – this will start her off on the path to sociability. At first, this can feel a bit silly – try starting with a running commentary on what you are doing 'look, I'm loading the washing machine... haven't you got lots of dirty clothes... the machine is going to make lots of whooshing noise in a minute...' Once you have done it for a while, you will feel less self-conscious, especially when you see how much your baby loves it.

Singing or saying nursery rhymes at this stage will encourage her to look for patterns in speech, and to answer back. As well as talking to your baby, look out for all her responses and involve her. Imitate the sounds your baby makes, interpreting them into speech. For example, when she goes 'oohh' while looking at you, you might reply 'oohh, hello. Are you saying hello? Yes, hello baby!'

At this stage, your baby is interested in people but because she has not yet grasped the concept that things continue to exist when out of sight (object permanence – see Chapter 14) she has not understood that there is one mother and one father who come and go, plus other people who may or may not be known to her. Once this happens she becomes more afraid of being separated and can develop fear of strangers, but right now she is fine with most people. So this is a good time to introduce her to lots of people, especially future childminders, nursery staff and so on. If your baby is going to be left with other people in the future, it is well worth starting her off now being left for short periods of time, so that they become known and familiar long before they are actually needed.

Games to play with your baby

Ticking game

Circling your finger on your baby's palm, saying:

'Round and round the garden, goes the teddy bear.'

Now walk your fingers up the inside of her arm in time to the next line,

'one step, two step,'

And reaching her armpit, say and do:

'TICKLE under there!'

Toe game

Wiggle each of your baby's toes in turn, starting with the big toe, and with the last toe – wee wee wee – run your fingers up her leg and tickle her tummy.

This little pig went to market
this little pig stayed at home
this little pig had roast beef
this little pig had none.
And this little pig went,
Wee, wee, wee
All the way home.

Clapping game

Clap your baby's hands inside your own. On the third line, tickle inside her palm, and draw a B shape, and fourth line, kiss her tummy.

Pat-a-cake, pat-a-cake, baker's man
Bake me a cake as fast as you can
Pat it and prick it and mark it with B
And put it in the oven for baby and me!

Developmental checks

Six to eight week check

Your health visitor will give your baby a check-up at six to eight weeks. This is in addition to the check-up your GP will give you, and it is important that your baby has this assessment, as it is designed to pick up any problems early on. For instance, in addition to the usual weight and growth checks, she will also test your baby's hearing and vision, heart and lungs, and will check for hip displacement and make sure that a baby boy's testes have descended properly. If problems are picked up at this stage they can often be remedied. Your health visitor will also talk to you about your baby's immunization programme.

It's a good idea to make a list of all the questions and worries that you have before you see your health visitor.

Your baby's growth

Typically in the first six months your baby will put on about one inch in length and half an inch of head circumference per month, plus around four to eight ounces per week, resulting in a doubling of birth weight by five to six months. These gains are average, so erratic growth week on week is quite normal.

Breast-fed or formula-fed – does it make a difference?

Breast-fed babies grow at different rates to formula-fed babies; generally speaking breast-fed babies tend to initially put on more weight but then become leaner and lighter whereas formula-fed babies tend to become heavier around this time. If you are charting your baby's growth in your Child Health Record book, then be aware that there are different charts for breast-fed or formula-fed babies, so you need to have the right one. A breast-fed baby's length and head circumference should, however, develop at the same rate as formula-fed babies. If your baby is putting on what appears to be too much or too little weight, it is important to talk to your health visitor.

It is rare that a breast-fed baby becomes overweight, but if your baby does, it is not sensible to put her on a diet; she will lose the weight when she becomes more active. Babies on formula who seem excessively chubby may need brand and dosage modified, in consultation with your health visitor.

The NHS throughout the UK now follows the World Health Organization's recommendations that solids are not introduced before six months, based on recent substantial research. Babies' guts are not normally mature enough to cope with anything other than milk before this age, and introducing solids early can lead to health problems later on. If your baby seems hungrier than usual, it may just be a temporary problem; she may be ill or teething for instance. Talk to a breastfeeding counsellor or your health visitor for more help.

Support for you

Getting support for you is important at this stage. You will probably still be at home full time with your baby, and while you may be enjoying her, you will need adult company too. Try to make the effort to meet up regularly with those people you met previously at post-natal support groups, Bumps and Babes or baby massage. It should be easier for you to get out of the house now, so you could meet in other locations, go for a walk in the park or go to the local shopping centre together. The change of scene will also be stimulating for your baby.

You might like to take your baby to your local mother and toddler group. Although she is not yet mobile, she will enjoy watching the toddlers, and there will be a large range of toys there, including several for non-mobile babies. Mother and toddler groups can vary tremendously in how they are run as they are usually just voluntary affairs, set up and maintained by parents who have a bit of spare energy! The best ones have a range of toys from construction toys like bricks, make-believe toys like pretend kitchens, and a good dressing-up box. They should also have paints, play dough and other creative materials set up for the children to enjoy. Some will have a sing-song session at the end.

Case study

Gordon and Heather have already noticed what their six-week-old baby Diana seems to like or dislike. She likes having lots of background noise: music, TV, the sound of the Hoover or listening to their voices. She starts to cry if the house is too quiet! She seems to dislike very bright lights and hates getting in the bath. Her parents wonder whether it's OK to have this noise on all the time, or should they try to get Diana used to peace and quiet too?

It's just great that Gordon and Heather have already worked out strategies for soothing Diana. Many babies seem to prefer some types of input over others, and it can take parents some time to discover what works best for their baby. It is also worth remembering that the womb was a pretty noisy place; continual booming from Heather's heartbeat, loud swooshing noises from the circulation and digestion – it can apparently reach 70 decibels in there, so it is not surprising that Diana is perturbed by silence. This may be why second babies can be calmer as they are born into noisier environments, having toddlers rushing around. There is no need to worry about getting her used to quiet; as the memory of the womb fades she will be less interested in stimuli that remind her of that place – in the meantime Gordon and Heather have some pretty good strategies for soothing Diana when she's fractious.

Fascinating baby facts

- At first your baby will close her eyes while feeding, unable to concentrate on two things at once, but by her third month she will feed with her eyes open, gazing at you.

- It has been estimated that if a baby continued to grow at the rate she does in the first year of life, by the time she reached adulthood she would be the height of Nelson's column!

- Her first tooth may appear around five to seven months of age. Drooling and red cheeks are often the first sign, but can occur several weeks before. Start brushing when her first tooth is through.

- At birth, it takes your baby between five and ten minutes to get used to something new, but by three months it will only take between 30 seconds and two minutes, and at the grand age of six months, your baby will cope in less than 30 seconds.

- Kissing has origins in primitive weaning. Before blenders, we would chew baby's food and then pass it from our mouth to her, like a kiss.

- 'Kissing it better' is an old tradition which symbolizes sucking out evil forces that cause pain.

- Parents instinctively use a special low-keyed rhythm of speech to attract and keep their baby's interest, which psychologists call 'Motherese'. Your baby will teach you to do this by her intense response when you use it. Many nursery rhymes have a similar quality: for instance, nearly all languages have a rhyme which sounds like 'Humpty Dumpty', i.e. a four-line stanza with four beats per line, and with a particular sing-songy quality. Try singing nursery rhymes to your baby and see how she responds.

- Babies are born with a sweet tooth and breast milk is sweet (far sweeter than cows' milk). This is probably why we adults revert to hot, sweet drinks when we feel ill or miserable.

05

the amenable baby – six months to toddling

In this chapter you will learn:
- about the exciting physical developments your baby makes at this stage
- how to help him speak
- why your baby becomes anxious about being separated from you.

For many parents, this stage of babyhood feels like the easiest. Your baby can sit up, and at around nine months he develops the ability to grasp objects between his fingers and thumb, so he gets pretty good at playing with toys, as well as being able to point at objects. Many parents don't really notice this ability emerging, but the use of the opposing thumb is one of the most important evolutionary developments to set us apart from other apes.

Now he really feels strong affection for you and for all his immediate family, but this means he hates separation, and it also means he is scared of strangers. To look at this in a positive light, one of the reasons this happens is that he has developed good communication skills with one or two people and is afraid of losing that, and so he is on the cusp of being able to communicate with lots of people. That ability to point is just the beginning of developing a large vocabulary, as you begin to talk to each other about the world about you.

Physical milestones

In this second six months, your baby's weight gain begins to slow down a bit so that now he is gaining about three to five ounces per week, and monthly his length changes by about half an inch, head circumference by a quarter of an inch. However you will probably find that you are less concerned about his weight now, the change to solid foods brings other things to think about, and his motor development – how and when he gets moving – is probably what you will focus on at this stage.

At seven months his finger control starts to get sophisticated, and he grasps objects between his thumb and finger. This is one of the most exciting developments he makes; using our 'opposing thumbs' is the main skill that separates us from the rest of the animal kingdom and which allows us to use tools. Your baby will now be able to pick up tiny things. Let him practise on finger foods, rather than things on which he could choke. He should, over these few months, develop control over his individual fingers, being able to poke at things with his index finger, holding things at first scissor fashion between finger and thumb which should then evolve into a definite pincer grasp.

As you will also be introducing your baby to solid foods at this stage, you can combine this weaning with fine finger control development. It is important your baby gets used to a variety of tastes and textures, and it is also vital that he controls his own intake and thus learns to recognize his 'satiation cues' – i.e. to know when he is full and to stop eating. Babies who have these cues overridden are more likely to be obese when they are older. The ideal way to manage this is to give your baby a variety of finger foods and let him pick and choose for himself. Thus he is in control of his appetite, and he is also practising his fine finger control. Even though he might get quite skilled at feeding himself, you should never leave your baby alone when he is eating.

A sample lunch might be:

- Small sandwiches, carrot or cucumber batons, cheese or ham cubes, apple segments, grapes cut in half, cooked pasta shells.

Lots of pointing and talking about things is important at this stage. You can also point at things in books together, and be sure to respond when he points at something by naming it, and then talking a bit more about it.

By eight months he can sit unaided and then lean forward to pick up toys. When he is on his tummy he might also discover that kicking pushes him along, although he will go backwards at first.

- You could encourage him to go the right way by putting an object just out of his reach.
- Think about the surface your baby is on; he will probably get moving more easily on carpet than wood floor for instance, because it is not as slippery.

Getting moving

The biggest variation for babies seems to be the age and the manner in which they get moving. Some will crawl on all fours, some will roll around the room, others will shuffle on their bottoms. There is some evidence that crawlers will walk earlier than bottom shufflers, but it is doubtful that you can coach your baby in these early movements. Better to leave them to it.

One researcher found that coaching helped babies walk earlier, but other researchers have not managed to duplicate this. However, putting your baby in a walker can slow down the time at which he starts to crawl, and every year there are accidents with baby walkers; so don't invest in one if you are hoping it will teach your baby to walk.

Somewhere around twelve months your baby may stand with you holding him. He then progresses to pulling himself up from sitting, eventually standing alone. When he tires, he sits down with a bit of a bump; one of the benefits of nappies!

- Arranging furniture so he can cruise round the room holding on will help him practise his walking skills.
- Once he starts to walk, don't rush out and buy shoes. These are unnecessary until he is walking confidently and needs protection outside. Indoors, use non-slip socks, or best of all, bare feet.

Establishing boundaries

Once he becomes mobile, even before he is walking, nothing will be safe and you need to put precious objects well out of reach or even packed away for a few years. He is naturally curious, which is a great thing, and you don't want to have to thwart him and say no all the time, so be selective in what you leave accessible. Having said that, you will need to establish boundaries and some things can be 'no' – plugs and electricals for instance, but remember that he is not capable of being naughty, he is just finding out about the world, so try not to get angry, and never leave him alone with something that is potentially dangerous.

- He can understand no, but doesn't realize for a long time that no can be permanent; he will just think it applies to that moment.

Helping him to develop independence

As your baby gets going he will veer between feeling adventurous and bold, and timid and uncertain. You are going to be his touchstone; he will take his cues from you, return to you as a safe base. Encourage your baby in independence: show him how to hold a spoon and use a cup. Think about arranging the house so he has his own space and own responsibilities, for instance you could give him a low peg so he can hang his own coat up, his own bookshelf which he can put his own books on and so on.

Although your baby is capable of sleeping through the night at this stage, there is no guarantee that he will be doing this, and many parents are still having disturbed nights well into the second year. Some babies, who have been sleeping well up till now, suddenly start having difficulties at this stage. One reason can be separation anxiety. Before six months your baby did not realize that you continued to exist when you were not there, but now that he has grasped this concept, it means he gets alarmed when you leave the room. That is why many babies try to prolong the bedtime routine or find it really hard to settle. This will pass with plenty of reassurance, but keep doing the same bedtime routine and keep the consistency going; if you respond by changing things or abandoning all attempts to settle him, he will assume that bedtimes don't matter and that he can stay awake as long as he wants, and at this age he really does need his sleep, no matter how lively he may appear!

Understanding the world around him – developing self-awareness

One of the ways babies are very different from adults is in the way they understand themselves, other people and the objects in the world around them. For the first six months they have to try and break the world down into different people, different objects; initially they cannot really tell where one thing begins and ends, your baby didn't understand that you are another person distinct from him who continues to exist in another place when he is not looking at you. He didn't understand that objects continue to exist when he can't see or hear them – as far as he is concerned 'out of sight is out of mind'.

At this stage however, he grasps the important concept of 'object permanence' and understands that objects continue to exist (see Chapter 14). This is why he takes great pleasure in dropping things and letting you retrieve them; it is as if he is causing the objects to come and go, when he didn't realize they could do that before. He also now understands that you are a permanent feature, that there is only one of you and you come and go but continue to exist when he can't see you. This is one of the reasons he becomes upset when you disappear, even though he did not fret before. Although he felt affection and love for you before, it was bound up in his feelings about himself and his reactions to what was happening to him. It took most of these first six or seven months to really become attached to you as a particular person, but now he can become afraid that you, his most important person, might disappear. He also knows how to communicate with you; you are the one who knows what he needs, what he is thinking, and the loss of that becomes terrifying. In addition, if a stranger approaches, he does not know how to communicate with this new person, he has not developed a communicational rapport with him, and so your baby becomes anxious.

This separation anxiety and its flip side, the fear of strangers, is a stage most babies pass through, and it is a compliment really; it tells you that your baby feels confident about communicating with you, believes that you are there for him and care for him. This stage will pass; in the meantime be gentle with your baby when meeting strangers. It will be far more positive if you can act as if everything is normal, talk to the person and smile at him, perhaps ask them to wait before approaching or interacting with your baby directly. In the meantime, your baby will be watching you carefully to see how you react, and if you seem positive, he will be more prepared to accept this new person.

Babies become self-aware sooner than we might think, although psychologists still can't agree when this happens. Very young babies love looking at themselves in mirrors, but they may not realize who they are looking at for quite some time. If you pop some lipstick on your baby's nose and then show him his reflection, it is not until about 15 months that he will touch his *own* nose when he sees it.

Tie a mirror to the bars of your baby's cot – he will love it.

Investigating what a baby might believe about himself is fairly difficult, but we do know that babies around nine to twelve months will look longer and smile more at pictures of themselves; and that by 15 to 18 months babies will talk about themselves for instance as 'baby', or use their own name to label pictures of themselves.

Show your baby pictures of himself and of other babies, and talk to him about what you are both looking at.

Communicating

By six months your baby should be using recognizable sounds and babbling with double syllables 'Aaa.eee'.

At seven months, he will add consonants to his repertoire, so you get 'mummmummmum'. You may notice that when he cries he seems to chat as well, changing the sound by using his tongue and lip movements in different ways.

- At this point you can help by turning his cooing sounds into words. Depending on what you do he will pause or vary the sound. If he sees you responding enthusiastically to mum, mum, mum for instance, he will do it more often, and gradually associate that sound with you.
- You can start teaching him non-verbal signals; like waving for bye-bye, arms open wide for big hug, nodding or shaking the head for yes or no.
- This is a good age to start baby-signing classes if you find this interesting. Babies do seem to progress faster at speaking if they have the opportunity to communicate with signs first.

> Signs that we all understand: Come here (beckoning finger), I/me (point to self), yes (nod), no (shake), don't know (shrug), quiet (finger to mouth), sleep (hands to side of head, eyes shut), time (pointing to wrist), stop (palm held up), OK (thumb and forefinger together).

At nine months, he discovers shouting, and for the first time he may use simple noises to mean something, e.g. Dada, ta-ta. He knows his own name, and understands a few other words.

Ten months is the 'joint attention stage' when your baby can concentrate on more than one thing at a time. Now his intellect will grow in leaps and bounds, and he will benefit greatly from you pointing things out and telling him about them, as he will be able to concentrate on your words and what you are pointing to, at the same time.

Eleven months is the average age for a first word, but then there is a long delay before any more words appear at around 15 months. Many parents never notice this first word, as it may not sound very clear, but as far as your baby is concerned 'da' means cat and he has used that particular sound to represent that black and white creature who lives in his house, and that is in fact the definition of a word.

Throughout this stage he will need lots of encouragement, and with positive reinforcement he will become a chatterbox, and love to strike up conversations with everybody he meets. For this to progress beyond 'toddler conversation' so that he can grow up to feel confident and to have the natural inclination to talk to others, you need to give him plenty of practice. Listen to him, talk back, and value what he says. At the same time, try to improve his listening skills through games. Teach him not to interrupt and to take turns. Begin to demonstrate good manners – say please, thank you and pardon to him as you would to others.

It is extremely important that you are positively encouraging his attempts to speak. No matter how clumsy or inarticulate he sounds, you need to be delighted with his efforts. Children whose parents correct what they say are easily put off and stop trying to communicate. The best way to teach your child to speak is to do what is called 're-casting' – giving your baby alternative ways of talking about the object. So repeat what he says, but expand and 're-cast' or re-word it.

For example, see this conversation between Sandra and Natalie, a perfect example of scaffolding:

Dah

What are you saying to me?

Dah

Oh yes, that *is* a car! Clever girl! It is *our* car! We are going to get in it now!

Crying

By now it should be relatively easy for you to work out why your baby is crying compared to the earlier months, and his crying should be a more deliberate communication; he may cry to attract your attention and then wait for you to come and help.

However there will also be times when he cries through distress; for instance at meeting strangers, or when something alarms him, and then he will need comforting and cuddling just as much as he did in his first few months. He may also have difficulty sleeping and wake up crying; again his fears are real and can't be rationalized or ignored, but will need comfort and help. He is still not yet able to manipulate you or cry to get his own way; this won't happen until a bit later, when he is toddling. Although he is crying to get a response from you and this may on occasions look like manipulation, he is really not capable yet of that level of planning and forethought, and his emotions are still very immediate and overwhelming, needing you to help him calm down.

Games to play with your baby

At this stage, singing together is a great way for your child to grasp the rhythm and turn-taking of language. You might want to join a music group, or your local parent and toddler group may well have a music session.

Action songs to do together:

Row your boat

Sit on the floor facing your baby, hold both his hands firmly in yours, and rock backwards and forwards as if you were rowing a boat together:

> Row, row, row your boat,
> Gently down the stream.
> Merrily, merrily, merrily, merrily,
> Life is but a dream.

Ring o'roses

Dance round in a circle with your baby in your arms and fall down on the last line. For babies who can stand, hold both his hands and slowly circle, both falling down on the last line. This will help the baby who is pulling himself to standing but not yet managing to let go and sit down again:

> Ring a ring o' roses
> A pocket full of poses
> A-tishoo, a-tishoo
> We all fall down!

You can also provide rudimentary musical instruments at this time: bells, shakers and things to drum on – old saucepans are good for this. Make your own maracas by filling a small round plastic pot with gravel.

This is also a good age at which to introduce quiet time together reading books. Sturdy picture books are best, and you should sit your baby on your lap and slowly turn the pages, talking about each picture. Encourage your baby to point at the things he knows.

Good toys for six to twelve months are stacking cups, shape sorters, and anything you can put things in and out of. Water play is excellent at this stage; sand is also good once he has stopped putting everything in his mouth.

Support for you

If you are still at home full-time with your baby, then hopefully this stage feels not too taxing. You are used to being a parent, your baby has a more predictable pattern, you are communicating well, and he should be sleeping through the night. It is still useful though, to get out and about, as this will not only give you some adult company, it will also provide extra stimulation for your baby, and meeting a range of people while still with you is very helpful for moving through that 'fear of strangers' stage.

You will not be having any developmental checks at this stage unless there are particular concerns about your baby, but you can still call on your health visitor at her clinic for advice on diet and weaning, and to check that your baby is progressing satisfactorily. She may then be able to tell you about other groups in your area. At this stage you might want to attend baby-signing classes, which most parents find an enjoyable way of enhancing communication with their babies. There are often various singing groups for mothers and babies, and this is an ideal age to attend these, when your baby is alert and interested but before he starts racing around, unable to sit still! If he is very physical and interested in getting moving, then there may be a soft play area locally where you can go and let him roll around in safety. Tumble Tots, for instance, may be something you are interested in attending now.

Case study

Jessica's big sister Annie just loves watching Teletubbies, and if her parents William and Holly let her, she would spend all day in front of her favourite DVD. Recently Holly has noticed that Jessica smiles and points at the TV when the smiley sun comes on, and wonders if it is possible that Jessica, at only nine months, can recognize that the sun has a face like hers?

Jessica at nine months probably does see this baby face as 'like me' though how far she really understands consciously what this means is open to interpretation. But it does seem true that children can recognize who is of a similar age to themselves very early on, and are fascinated by their peers. They simply lack the social skills to make any advances to other children without adult help.

Fascinating older baby facts

- Babies whose mothers talk to them a lot are more likely to be brighter toddlers.

- You can tell what sort of child your toddler will be by the way he learns language. If he starts by naming objects word by word, he will be an abstract thinker. If he prefers social phrases like hello, bye-bye or oh dear, he is more likely to be sociable.

- When babies are full, they turns their head away, and this is the origin of shaking our head 'no'.

- Sticking out your tongue is seen as rude because it symbolizes the way babies reject food.

- Within 12 months your baby will have gained about eight inches (20 centimetres) and will be about three times as heavy as when he was born.

- Each generation is on average taller than previous. Your children will probably be taller than you; today's boys are about three centimetres taller than their fathers and girls about two centimetres taller than their mothers.

section two

special situations

Introduction

In the previous section, we looked at what to expect from your baby at each stage of development, but the particular timings only applied to babies born at term. Premature babies will develop in the same way as term babies and go through the same stages, but will reach each stage at a later age. This section looks at what particular effects being born premature will have on your baby.

As most twins and multiples are also born premature, it seems sensible to consider their particular development in this section too; though twins are also affected socially and emotionally by being one of two, and we look here at some of the particular effects twinhood has on your babies.

Generally speaking though, twins and premature babies develop in similar ways to term singleton babies, and this section will just highlight the particular differences for them. If your baby is not premature or one of a twin, then you can skip this section. If you have twins then it is worth reading both chapters, as twins are often premature, and multiple births would definitely be born early.

What you will find is that for special babies like premature babies or twins and multiples, your input is vital, and there are lots of things you can do to help.

premature babies

In this chapter you will learn:
- why some babies are born prematurely
- how you are likely to feel about your premature baby
- what you can do to help your premature baby develop.

In times past, babies who were born very early were not expected to survive and would have been defined as late miscarriages. However, recent advances in medicine mean that we can now keep babies alive earlier and earlier, and the prognosis improves for these babies all the time.

What do we mean by premature?

Your pregnancy is measured from the date of onset of the last period. This is not, of course, the date your baby was conceived, which is on average two weeks after this, but as this is the only event the medical profession can be absolutely sure of, pregnancy is usually counted from that day. Babies are usually born anywhere between 38 and 42 weeks after that and are defined as premature if born before 37 weeks; before 32 weeks they are referred to as very pre-term infants (VPI).

Reasons for prematurity

With some pregnancies it is obvious why the baby has been born early: twins and triplets often come early as they run out of room; some babies are artificially induced early due to complications such as pre-eclampsia. But about one third of all premature births are unexplained. We know that stress or anxiety in pregnancy can lead to premature birth or low birth weight, and this might be because adrenalin can trigger uterine contractions. We also know that first-born children are often smaller and lighter at birth, and are more likely to be premature.

How you might feel about your premature baby

Your overwhelming feeling initially is likely to be shock. Shock that your baby has arrived before you were really ready and shock at the appearance of your baby. You were probably expecting a chubby baby with a healthy colour, just like the idealized images in the baby magazines; instead you have a scrawny, skinny little baby, perhaps with translucent skin, or covered in down. She does not look like a baby – you might even feel revulsion for her, which then makes you feel guilty!

In addition the birth probably felt traumatic – you were not prepared for it, there may have been attempts to stop it; it felt like a medical emergency instead of the rite of passage you were hoping for. However it went, you probably felt out of control, and the more that women feel in control of their births, the easier they find it to come to terms with as an experience.

Many parents talk about feeling out of control for quite some time. There is the lack of control in the unexpected birth, and then instead of taking your baby home, she is transferred to a special care baby unit (SCBU) where other people are responsible for her. You may not feel you have permission to relate to your baby, it is almost as if she is not your baby, but belongs to the unit.

How you feel about your baby is thus more complicated than for parents with full-term babies. If your baby had been born at term your relationship would have begun when you first met and would develop as a result of the interactions between you, but with a premature baby you are one step removed, and how you feel about your baby is going to be influenced by your own internal worries and states rather than by the baby and what she does. Other people feed into this too – if they are acting with worry or even rejection, it is easy to internalize this far more than if you were holding your baby and developing that relationship yourself. You are trying to form a relationship one step removed.

Some parents want to distance themselves from their baby as they are scared that she will die and are seeking to protect themselves emotionally, but most parents who have been through this situation will say that this strategy is not helpful, even if the baby does eventually die. They say that they were better able to come to terms with their baby's death if they felt they did everything they could to make the baby's short life bearable, with love and touch and affection.

Special care baby units (SCBUs)

Neonatal units are strange places full of frightening equipment but try to bear in mind that all this technology is vitally necessary for keeping your baby alive and also in helping her to grow and develop outside the womb.

Parents do not usually feel comfortable in SCBUs, at least not at first. The medical staff focus on the babies, they don't always have time to explain what they are doing and while some will be welcoming and accommodating, others can act as if you the parents are in the way. Their priority is keeping your baby alive, and while of course this is what we all want, having had nine months where you were centre of attention as parents to be, to suddenly be sidelined can feel quite alienating. And going home from hospital after the birth leaving your baby behind is a terrible experience; you have nothing to do but run over your memories again and again – this can be quite overwhelming.

Having to gear your days around visits to the SCBU is a real strain. This is a good time to ask for help from other people with tasks like providing meals, shopping, washing and cleaning as you will simply not have time to do all this. If you have other children you also need to make sure that you have time for them.

Helping your premature baby while in a SCBU

Your premature baby will especially benefit from breast milk; apart from containing all the nutrients she needs to grow, it will protect her against neonatal necrotizing enterocolitis – an often fatal disease which affects formula-fed premature babies. Expressing little and often is the best way to get the supply going, and dual pumping with an electric breast-pump day and night is probably the most efficient way to express. Contact a breastfeeding counsellor for more help, and to access an electric pump to use at home (there are reduced or free rates for babies in special care). Your baby will probably not be able to breast-feed at first; the reflexes needed for breastfeeding mature later, with rooting occurring before suckling so your baby may look for the breast but be unable to co-ordinate the sucking and swallowing needed once she gets there.

- Make sure you ask for plenty of help with establishing a breastmilk supply.
- Ask if your hospital can use donor breastmilk instead of formula, which is better for your baby.
- Contact NCT breastfeeding counsellors for support through this difficult time.

Even though your baby might not seem very responsive, she will still be aware of you; she will know your voices, and she needs to get to know your touch and smell just as a full-term newborn baby does.

Premature babies as young as 25 weeks post-conception respond to touch, and gentle forms of physical contact are good for premature babies. Check with the staff what is possible, but even your very small premature baby will benefit from hand-holding and gentle stroking.

There are also huge benefits for your baby from 'kangaroo care'. This is where you hold your baby upright with her naked skin next to your naked skin; usually you tuck her inside your shirt next to your bare chest. Babies who have kangaroo care are better able to maintain their body temperatures, sleep better, cry less, breath more regularly, breastfeed for longer, gain weight faster and are discharged from hospital earlier than those without this type of contact. In addition, parents who give their babies kangaroo care express greater confidence in themselves as parents.

Infant massage helps too; premature babies who have regular massage gain weight faster, perform better on tests, and can leave hospital earlier. Ask one of the neonatal nurses to show you the best way to massage your baby.

Finally, your premature baby will benefit from vestibular stimulation just as full-term babies do; they need rocking, swinging and being carried. Babies who are given extra vestibular stimulation gain weight faster, are less irritable, breathe more regularly, move less jerkily, sleep more and spend more time in quiet alert states than pre-terms who are not given extra vestibular stimulation.

The developmental progress of premature babies

The womb is obviously the best place to grow, and being outside the womb is going to compromise your baby, but neonatal medicine is making tremendous advances all the time, not only in keeping younger and younger babies alive, but also in making the prognosis more positive.

Traditionally SCBUs were normal hospital environments, with lots of noise and bright lights 24/7. It is now recognized that premature babies do better if their environment is more womb-like, and efforts are made in most neonatal units to keep adverse stimulation to a minimum. For instance, attempts are made to keep the incubators quieter and darker, with the babies resting in the foetal position nestling on lambskins or on waterbeds or even on hammocks; all of these surfaces mean that when they move they feel gentle resistance and get the same sort of feedback as they would in the womb, as well as getting some vestibular sensation. These small changes help the babies gain weight faster, sleep and breathe more easily and generally be less restless and irritable than babies in standard incubators. The babies who have this more realistic environment also stay healthier, develop more rapidly and score higher on later IQ tests than those in the traditional SCBU.

Given the recent advances, some of the research findings which predicted poor outcomes for premature babies may well be out of date. Most premature babies have no disabilities or ongoing problems at all, though the earlier they are born, the more likely it is that there will be problems. However, many of these will be fairly mild and can be overcome with treatment. Even though premature babies can survive earlier and earlier births, they still will mostly grow up to be fine.

Of babies born at 31 weeks or later, 98 per cent will survive, but babies born earlier than this are at risk of many problems including visual, hearing, motor deficits, poor emotional regulation, attention problems and language delays. Of babies born at 28 weeks, 10 per cent will have a significant disability, and 20–30 per cent of babies born around 24/25 weeks will have a significant disability, but if you turn that around, it means that 90 per cent of babies born at 28 weeks will have only mild or even no problems.

A British study called EPICure followed 300 babies born before 26 weeks and found that around half (51 per cent) had no problems at all. A quarter (26 per cent) had only mild problems like hearing difficulties or short-sightedness but the remaining quarter (23 per cent) had severe disabilities including cerebral palsy (3–6 per cent of premature babies), seizures and blindness. Around a quarter of babies born weighing less than 1,000 g (2 lbs 3 oz) will have problems with sight for instance, but this can vary from a mild squint through to blindness. Babies born very early may also have a problem with hearing as their hearing is still maturing at 24–26 weeks. It doesn't help that some SCBUs can be very noisy places.

It is important to keep an eye on how your baby is developing once you have her home; make sure she gets hearing and sight checks regularly.

Babies who are less than 1,500 g at birth (3 lbs 5 oz) perform more poorly at school and have been found to be about six points lower on IQ tests, but remember that 85–115 is average intelligence, so six points lower is not particularly significant, and being in a stimulating home environment can more than compensate for this.

Your premature baby can catch up if you can spend time stimulating and interacting with her. Make this your priority when you get your baby home.

When your baby comes home

Even though your premature baby has to overcome all sorts of odds to survive, and even if at the very beginning it looked as if she would never be a 'normal' baby, as we shall see later in this book, your baby's brain is very flexible and able to adapt to all sorts of situations. If you can provide a stable, loving home with plenty of stimulation, you will really help minimize any possible disadvantages she might have had from being born too early.

In addition, there should also be lots of follow-up help available to you, and it is important that you take advantage of this. Regular hearing and eye checks for instance can put right difficulties before they affect your baby significantly. Speech therapy will be available if needed and so on.

It is very tempting to compare your child's progress with other children, but in order to be fair you must compare her to children at the same developmental age rather than birth age. She will still go through all the developmental stages that her contemporaries go through, but these may mature later, and this is natural and normal. For instance, premature babies begin to smile six weeks after they *should* have been born. Many other developmental sequences will unfold as your baby's brain reaches a certain stage – but they do all get there eventually, and premature babies do catch up. Babies who weigh less than 1,000 g (2 lbs 3 oz) at birth will probably not catch up until they are about four or five years old.

Many parents say that they find keeping a diary of their babies' achievements helps them see how far they've come. One mother stated how much it helped to take a photograph of him the same time each week so she had a visual record of his progress, and was pleasantly surprise to see how much he was coming on.

Summary of this chapter

- Most premature babies will develop absolutely normally, though they will take longer to reach certain milestones, and some may be school age before they catch up with their peers.
- There are lots of things you can do to help your baby while she is in a SCBU so liase with the staff and make sure you are doing as much as you can.
- Because babies' brains are so flexible, having a stimulating home environment will more than compensate for a premature birth.
- Record your baby's progress week by week, in diary, photo or video format – and this will be encouraging as you see how quickly she progresses.

What this means for you and your baby

Despite all the disadvantages your premature baby might appear to have, hang on to the fact that your input can make all the difference. Try to make your baby your priority – while she is in hospital, spend time with her using kangaroo care, baby massage and vestibular stimulation. As much breastmilk as possible is best.

Once your baby is home, she will need help, extra stimulation and lots of interacting, but all this will help your baby catch up.

07

twins

In this chapter you will learn:
- how twinning happens
- what parenting twins and multiples feels like
- how twins develop.

Twins are endlessly fascinating. Whole books have been written about them, and many urban myths have sprung up about twins. A twin would be a soul mate, someone who knows you absolutely, with whom you might have a secret language. In our society twins are perhaps a little idealized, and the result is that parenting twins can be quite a shock when the reality kicks in. As we shall see, twins can vary tremendously in how well they get on, and in the early months in particular, twins are unlikely to relish that special bond.

How twins happen

There are lots of misconceptions about how twins are made, but there are basically only two ways you might have conceived twins, although many twins are now produced as the result of assisted conceptions. The most likely reason for having twins without assistance is that the mother released two eggs at the same time instead of one, both of which were fertilized. This results in non-identical twins who will be genetically no more alike than ordinary siblings, and statistically speaking, there is a 50/50 chance that they will be the same sex. These twins are called dizygotic (or fraternal).

Less commonly, one egg splits in two shortly after it has been fertilized, and grows into two, genetically identical, foetuses (obviously the same sex). Such twins are called monozygotic (or identical).

Twins from assisted conceptions will nearly always be dizygotic.

The only way of knowing for sure whether your twins are genetically identical is through a blood test. It used to be thought that non-identical twins have separate placentas, but these sometimes fuse, so having only one placenta is not necessarily a sure sign. In addition, identical twins have been born in separate sacs, probably because the splitting happened later.

In the UK, one in every 90 births results in two or more babies (meaning that one in 40 children are twins), but less than one in every 250 births produces identical twins. Monozygotic twinning is entirely random, but you are more likely to conceive fraternal twins if you have frequent sexual intercourse (hence the fact that there were more twins in the UK after the end of the Second World War, and that twins are more likely in the first few months after marriage). Twins are also more likely if either you or your partner already has twins in the family, although the maternal side is stronger. The likelihood of fraternal twins also increases as the mother approaches her late thirties, and the more children you already have, the more likely subsequent ones will be twins. Some races are more likely to have twins than others: Nigerian mothers have the highest twinning rates, mothers with Oriental backgrounds have the lowest rate, Caucasians are in between.

Although live twins are relatively rare, with the development of ultrasound we have come to realize that twin pregnancies are quite common, but most twins die in the womb, usually before the 12th week of pregnancy. About one in eight of all natural pregnancies begin as twins but only 2 per cent of these will result in twins at birth.

Multiple births, like triplets, quads or more, are even rarer, although common over the last few years due to assisted conception, such as the use of IVF or fertility drugs. Most doctors now will encourage parents who have artificially conceived more than two babies to abort the extra foetus, as the chances of the pregnancy being viable are slim, and the developmental outcomes for more than two babies is often poor. In fact, some clinics now insist parents agree beforehand to abort any extra foetuses before proceeding with treatment, which means that births of more than two will return to those previous, extremely infrequent, rates.

If you are indeed due to have more than two babies, then you will need a lot of extra help and support, both while the babies recover in a SCBU (see previous chapter) and afterwards, when looking after three babies at the same time at home. Most of the issues that apply to twins will also apply to you, but more so, with the added complication of extreme prematurity.

Getting ready for twins

For twins, 37 weeks is considered full term and 2500 g (5 lbs 6 oz) is an average twin weight. So already you can see that twins start life at a slight disadvantage to singletons even if they reach term, but in fact twins are far more likely to be premature, with all the attendant difficulties that entails (see previous chapter). Ten per cent of all premature births are twins, and half of all twin births are caesarean section. Twin births can be straightforward if the babies are not very pre-term and are both well positioned but there are bound to be many more people in the delivery room and interventions are far more likely. Twins may grow at different rates in the womb, and it is not unusual to give birth to twins of very different sizes, even monozygotic twins.

If you are expecting twins you will need to be preparing for an early birth and may well have premature babies to cope with. In addition, it is far more likely that you will have a caesarean birth, and recovering from major abdominal surgery like this takes far longer than recovering from a straightforward vaginal delivery. It is probably helpful to assume that you are going to need a lot of help in the first six weeks just to recover from the effects of the birth.

Once the babies are here, you are going to be extremely busy, so take time beforehand to set up your support networks. Find out if there is a local twins club; they're a great source of information, support and equipment (contact Tamba for more details – see the Taking it Further section). There is no doubt that twins will cost more; you may need a bigger car or have to rearrange your home, but try to prioritize spending on extra help for several weeks, if not months, after the birth. If family cannot help out consider paying for extra help with cleaning and laundry, and get used to Internet shopping if you are not already au fait with this. In the weeks after the birth, all you can expect of yourself is to look after the babies; everything else will have to be delegated to someone else.

If you already have other children, be aware that their noses will be even more out of joint when twins arrive. Not only will you have far less time for them, visitors will make a huge fuss of these new arrivals and singleton siblings can feel really neglected.

If you can afford paid help during those first few months, view it as money well spent. If not, local Nursery Nurse colleges are always on the look out for twin families to give their students unpaid work experience – giving you an extra pair of hands. Your health visitor may also know of other similar schemes, which could provide you with assistance.

What do I need to buy?

- Try to borrow or hire expensive equipment such twin prams or buggies, but only use a reliable source. Your local twins club should be able to help and may have suggestions about the best makes. In the early days your babies may be able to share a cot or carry cot.
- Make a list of things you think you need, but don't rush out and buy everything – wait to see what you are given or lent. Look for second-hand clothes; NCT nearly-new sales are a good place to shop.

Your feelings

The first few weeks with just one new baby can be overwhelming; expect it to be doubly so when there are two to look after. Getting out of the house is a major expedition, and mothers of twins can quickly become isolated, which is probably one of the reasons they are more likely to have post-natal depression.

It's normal for new mothers to feel tired but, for you, parenthood started after a particularly draining time. During pregnancy the body has to work doubly hard to grow twin babies and carry them around. Then there are the effects of a complicated and highly medicalized birth. After all this you really need a good rest, but instead two tiny babies are depriving you of your normal amount of sleep. If they're in Special Care, that's additional mental strain and worry.

Crying babies are hard to handle; for you this will be doubly difficult as you inevitably leave one baby to cry while you deal with the other. Try to accept that you cannot be constantly available to each baby and that as long as you can answer their needs eventually, they will cope, just like second babies in other families.

It's also difficult to fall in love with two people at once. You will probably find that you have stronger feelings for one particular baby, which is perfectly normal. Your twins may look very different, they may be discharged from hospital at different times, they will certainly have different temperaments, and you may find one easier to cope with than the other. Be aware of this and try to make an effort to ensure that each twin gets interaction and affection from people around them.

'Special' babies

If your twins resulted from fertility treatment you could face turbulent emotions. Trying to conceive, you constantly reaffirmed that you want children. After all that sacrifice, your babies feel very 'special'. You might have an idealistic view of yourself as a parent.

However, all babies cry, stay awake at night and need frequent feeding. It can feel hard to admit that things are tough when your friends and family know what you went through to conceive your babies. Remember, you have as much right to feel depressed and in need of support as any other parent.

After those difficult early months, life does get easier. At about nine months they will begin to play together. They may entertain each other when they wake up, letting you lie in a bit. Although they create more work, this can eventually be offset by their ability to help each other.

How twins develop

Twins are just like any other babies; they want to be interacted with, fed and held. Initially they are not particularly interested in each other, and like all babies are drawn to adults, seeking to make that primary attachment and to develop that intimate early communication (see Chapters 09 and 15).

The problem for parents is that it's impossible to interact with two people at the same time in the way that babies want to be interacted with; to do that close mutual eye contact and exchanging smiles. Many twins therefore start out competing for parents' attention, and will cry loudly if they are not getting that undivided attention – so initially, if they are aware of each other, it's as competition. Studies have shown that even early on twins can be acutely jealous of each other. As they get older they may well fight a lot, so if you had this idealistic picture of cute children adoring each other, the reality can be a bit disheartening. Territories are often a source of dispute, and some twins will need their own space, and their own possessions.

Eventually though, as the main constant in each other's life, twins often become attachment figures for each other (see Chapter 09). One study looked at how twins felt about being separated from their mother aged 12 to 15 months, and found that the monozygotic babies did not protest at separation from their mothers but only protested at separation from each other. The twins had formed a strong 'horizontal' attachment with each other. However, this was not as marked in dizygotic pairs.

Why does this happen? Because getting around with twins is so much harder, parents tend to stay around the house more, often in the same room, and so for the early months and years, before they start nursery or school, twins are seldom apart and often have to rely on each other for comfort, entertainment and so on, far more so than other siblings. They tend therefore to develop a heightened awareness of each other, and it is suggested that monozygotic twins become even more sensitive to each other as they probably are already generally more similar. This heightened awareness probably explains that telepathic link that is so often attributed to twins.

Initially they may resist this close contact; some twins, particularly dizygotic, hate being in the same cot for instance. Monozygotic twins might be more compatible for co-sleeping, perhaps because they were less separate in the womb and therefore perhaps more accustomed to each other's movements. Also their sounds and smells will be more similar and therefore more familiar and probably more comforting.

- Try to respect your babies' need for personal space. When one or both twin gets distressed by contact with the other, allow them time out and space.
- Your twins will really benefit from having time alone with you, even if it is for just a few minutes each day. In fact, making the effort to give each twin individual attention and affection will make them more independent and less clingy as they know you are there and you care for them as an individual.

Language development in twins

As we shall see, language development relies on early interaction between primary caregiver and child – the proto-conversations that mothers spend so much time involved in before their babies start to talk (see Chapter 15). But mothers of twins have less time for this, and their interactions will tend to be shorter and more to the point. Twins usually have some language delay being about six months behind singletons, and tend to utter their first words later, speak in shorter and simpler sentences, have more limited vocabulary and have immature forms of expression for longer than singletons. Having said that, twins perform better on speech and language tests when they are together as they tend to be used to communicating with each other or as a pair.

You may well find that one twin is quieter or perhaps a little behind the other twin in speaking, and your tendency is also to address both twins together: 'Would you like a biscuit', 'Shall we go out now?' – you will not tend to ask each twin these questions separately, and the tendency will be for the more dominant or more advanced twin to answer for both of them.

Try to make sure each twin has time on their own interacting with an adult, even if just for a few minutes each day, from early on. This will help their language development. This could be something their father takes on as a particular task.

Twin language – idioglossia

Many twins (up to 40 per cent) develop a private language as they start to speak, and there is no harm in this as long as they are also acquiring normal language at the same time. What seems to happen is that because twins are in the unique situation of having another equally poor speaker to model their language on (as opposed to say an older sibling), they will tend to reinforce each other's mispronunciation, and as they spend so much time together, these mispronunciations become ways of communicating with each other.

If your twins are spending a lot of time in this private language, it is a sign that they are not having enough verbal input in other ways, so you will need to make more of an effort to communicate with each one individually. Having a reading time together each day may help, and perhaps each parent could read a bedtime story to each twin.

Development of a sense of self

The development of a sense of self (see Chapter 14) may come later for twins. Children generally recognize themselves in the mirror by 2½ years of age, and dizygotic twins do likewise, however monozygotic twins may take much longer – when they see the image in the mirror they usually think it is their twin. Around age three, for some as late as four, they begin to realize that what they are seeing is an image of themselves, not their twin, and often become confused as for the first time they realize that they look the same as their twin. You may have your child asking questions like, 'Is she me?' or 'Who am I?' or more poignantly, 'Is that why everyone looks at us?'

Identical twins often find it hard to develop separate identities from each other if they are never apart, and at some point you might need to help with this.

- Try, if you can, to get in the habit of always organizing some time alone with each baby each day. If relatives come to help, ask them to play with each baby in turn.

- Give them their own possessions; and they don't always need to have the same things as each other. One can have a train and one a lorry, one can have a doll with blond hair, the other brown and so on.

- Try not to treat them as a unit – they are two unique individuals.

Twins and birth order

Twins tend to respond according to their overall place within the family. If they have one older sibling, they will both exhibit characteristics of a second born. If they themselves are the oldest, they will adopt some traits of first-borns. However, the effect of being a twin is probably stronger than the effect of birth order. One twin is usually dominant in the relationship regardless of the order in which they were born.

Fascinating facts about twins

- Psychologists study twins to work out whether our personalities are inherited. Twins who were separated at birth often have astonishingly similar voices, gestures, and opinions – even choices of career!

- 25 per cent of identical twins are mirror images of each other.

- Left-handedness is twice as common for twins.

- The Yoruba tribe in Nigeria has the highest rate of twinning in the world due to consumption of a particular yam high in oestrogen. One in 11 people are a twin.

- Feydor Vasilet, a nineteenth-century Russian peasant, had 69 children – 16 twins pairs, seven triplets and four quadruplets.

- Being one of a multiple is perilous – there are only ten living sets of sextuplets in the entire world.

- The largest numbers of identical children were the Dionne quintuplets from Canada. Another set of quintuplets, from Argentina, consists of a pair of identical twin boys and a set of identical triplet girls.

section three

how your baby develops

Introduction

So far we have been looking at particular situations: having premature babies or twins, or with term babies, seeing how they develop at each particular stage. We have only been focusing on what your baby does; in this section we look more at why your baby does what she does, thereby giving you a more theoretical understanding of how your baby develops overall.

As you saw in Chapter 01, your baby's development unfolds as an interaction between her genes and environment. Her genes tell her what to do and roughly when to do it, but the fine-tuning of her skills happens in an environment that consists mainly of you. Part One of this section explains how your baby develops emotionally: what the effect of being part of a family has on her, how she learns to love, but also how she bonds with you and her family, and what the effect of bonding will have on her throughout her life. Part Two will then look at your baby's intellectual development: how she uses the world to make discoveries and to learn, and just what your role is in all of this.

Chapter 08 starts by explaining how human evolution resulted in babies being born too early, but shows how this is an advantage in that babies can thus adapt to the environment in which they are born. It goes on to explain that the important bits of your baby's brain – those which make her truly human – develop after she is born and only really mature with the right input from you. It thus shows you just why love matters to your baby. Chapter 09 looks at how this love unfolds during the first year, how your baby develops deep emotional attachments with the people who look after her – what we often call 'bonding'. It also looks at the consequences for not bonding with your baby, and how this causes problems, not only for our children, but for society in general. You will also find out how to make sure your baby does grow up to be an emotionally secure person. Chapter 10 looks at the ramifications of all of this for the childcare you choose for your baby and Chapter 11 looks at the effect of family structure on your child's sense of security.

We then move on, in Chapter 12 to consider the effect on your baby of having siblings, and in Chapter 13 we look to the future, to see how your parenting styles will affect your baby, and how you should parent your baby as she grows up.

So Part One will show you that your baby depends on you for social and emotional growth; in Part Two you will see that she also depends on you to grow and develop intellectually.

This sounds like a huge challenge, but in fact as long as you take time to get involved with your baby, she will show you what she needs, and that you will naturally do what is right for your baby's development.

Chapter 14 explains how babies' brains develop in the first year or so, how your baby understands what she experiences, and how her mental processes develop so that she can build up a body of knowledge. You will discover how your baby learns, and what you can do to help. Chapter 15 looks at why languages are so difficult to learn, and how your baby does this in such a short space of time. It also shows you just how much your baby is communicating before she actually produces any recognizable words. Chapter 16 will explain how play fits into your baby's intellectual development, the sorts of toys your baby will need, and why getting involved with books is useful at this stage. Finally Chapter 17 highlights the differences and similarities between boys and girls.

The first year of your baby's life is a huge challenge. Both you and your baby have such a lot to learn; hopefully this part of the book will make this entertaining and rewarding for both of you.

part

one

emotional development

08

the physical development of the social baby

In this chapter you will learn:

- that all babies are born too early
- how your baby's brain develops in a social world
- what you can do to help your baby's brain to grow.

One of the most remarkable things about a newborn baby is just how helpless she seems at first and how long she will be dependent on adults just to survive.

Some mammal babies, like the ruminants (those who eat grass, i.e. cows, horses, sheep etc.) get straight to their feet and start walking about. Others, like the cache mammals (who live in litters, i.e. kittens, puppies etc.) are born blind and helpless, but it's still only a matter of weeks till they are independent. Even compared to other apes, our babies are immature at birth and stay dependent for longer. Although chimpanzees and gorillas have similar length pregnancies (228 days and 256 days respectively compared to 267 days for humans), their babies will be fully mature by 11 years of age.

Babies are born too early

Scientists now think that while walking upright does give us lots of advantages, for instance it frees our hands for carrying things or using tools, the downside is that our pelvises need to be fairly narrow, and this restricts how big our newborn babies' heads can be.

In addition, being more intelligent than other species is definitely an advantage because we can think and plan and use tools creatively, but being more intelligent means a bigger brain, and thus a bigger head. So in evolutionary terms, having a bigger head and walking on two feet are advantages that compete with the ability to give birth safely and easily.

The compromise that evolution came up with was to allow our babies to be born early. If we compare ourselves to other species, particularly our close relatives the apes, our babies should probably be born after 18 months gestation. Scientists call these nine months when the baby is growing outside the womb, 'exterogestation' or 'secondary altriciality'.

Mothers need help raising babies

Giving birth to babies with large heads meant that our ancestral mothers were quite vulnerable during delivery and often needed help from other women. Afterwards they then had a big task ahead, having to look after a baby who was, not only initially quite helpless, but would also be dependent on her for many years. In order for this to be possible, our species had to become social and co-operative (if we were not like this already); mothers could not do all this on their own.

Fascinating fact

The story of Adam and Eve might be about the evolution of the human race!

No other species appears to experience anywhere near the level of pain giving birth that we do – the result of this struggle to give birth to intelligent babies. It's interesting how the biblical story Genesis alludes to this: Adam and Eve ate from the tree of knowledge, and the punishment for this was that women would give birth in pain.

Are big brains really an advantage?

A big brain is not necessarily as much of an advantage as you might think. It takes a lot of energy to power it, and as we have seen, puts a mother at risk during birth. What a bigger brain does do for a species is allow it to be versatile.

Most creatures on the planet are specialists; whether they use a long nose to extract ants out of anthills or use a long neck to reach the leaves on the trees that other animals cannot reach, they are excellent at doing one thing – usually accessing one particular food, in fact. These specializations, though they may seem 'clever,' do not require intelligence.

However, nearly every evolutionary line of the vertebrate tree has produced some genuinely smart animals, and these smart creatures tend to be omnivores. In evolutionary terms, when there is lots of food available, most species prosper, but when food suddenly runs scarce, the specialists can get into trouble because they are not able to adapt quickly enough. This is where the big brained, versatile omnivorous species triumph, and isn't it interesting that human brain size increased rapidly during the ice ages, a time when food would have been incredibly hard to find?

How your baby's brain grows – it's all about connections

Although it looks as if 'exterogestation' might be a risky strategy for your baby, in fact it gives her a huge advantage. Having half of the pregnancy take place outside the womb means that your baby can be shaped to fit her environment, and for human beings, who are the most versatile creatures on the planet, this makes complete sense.

No other species of baby is likely to be born into such a choice of environments and social groups as the human being. Baby's brains are able to do the majority of their growing in the environment they find themselves in, thus allowing them to adapt as needed. At birth, the human baby's brain is only a quarter of its final size. Even our closest relative, the chimp, gives birth to babies with brains already 41 per cent of adult size. In that first year outside the womb, your baby's brain will double to become half its final size, and by age three, it will be three quarters its final size.

Not only are they growing at a tremendous rate, babies' brains are also much busier than ours. At around two years of age a toddler's brain's energy consumption has reached adult levels, even though it's still smaller, and at age three it is actually using twice the energy of an adult brain, remaining this busy until age nine or ten when energy use begins to decline back to reach adult levels around age 18.

What is your baby's brain doing that requires so much energy? It's setting up connections. At birth each neuron (brain cell) has around 2,500 synapses (connections) and these increase in number rapidly, reaching a peak at around two to three years of age when there are about 15,000 synapses per neuron, more than are present in the adult brain. After age three, the child's brain starts deleting all the connections which are not used, while the ones that carry the most messages get stronger and survive.

Baby's brain as potential

You could think of your baby as one big potential. All those connections waiting to be used, to be strengthened by experience, or pruned when not needed. Her brain connections operate on a 'use it or lose it' principle, like a muscle, only once the connection has gone, it has gone forever.

The first year of your baby's life is all about building up connections through experience, and as certain events occur over and over again, the same group of neurons are activated simultaneously, and thus life becomes more predictable. So eventually when your baby sees you coming to pick her up, she stops crying and waits, perhaps giving you a wonderful smile in the meantime.

Your input is vital, and a stimulating environment will help your baby's brain to grow.

What is stimulating for your baby is not necessarily what you might think of as stimulating. Remember that what your baby's brain is doing is forming connections based on experience, so in fact events which are repeated over and over are stimulating. And you probably want these to be positive! Some suggestions:

- When changing your baby's nappy, sing some lively action songs with her, like 'Round and round the garden' (see Chapter 04 for some examples).
- Blow raspberries on her tummy and pedal her legs when you are dressing her or changing her clothes.
- Try to get out of the house every day and do something like go for a walk in the park. Let her see the leaves moving in the wind, ducks on ponds. When the weather is not so good, then a walk around a shopping centre can be entertaining, though avoid hot, crowded shops.
- When you are doing your daily tasks, involve her. Go round the supermarket when she is alert and active and talk to her about the things on the shelves. Put her in a doorway bouncer or cradle chair when you are in the kitchen and talk to her about what you are doing.

As you can see you don't have to give yourself extra tasks, but simply involve her in the things you are doing already. What she will enjoy is the interaction with you. So putting her in front of the TV or leaving her in a room with the radio on is not stimulating, but will in fact encourage her to tune out of conversation as she gets no response to her own efforts to communicate.

How love helps your baby's brain to grow

In order to double in size in that first year, your baby's brain needs an enormous increase in glucose metabolism, and this is partly triggered by a biochemical response to a loving parent.

Parents and babies spend a lot of time in what psychologists call 'mutual gaze' (staring at each other if you like) and when a woman (or a man who is also a father) looks at a baby, their pupils dilate, a sign of pleasure. So when your baby looks at you and sees your dilated pupils, her own nervous system becomes aroused in response, her own heart rate goes up and she releases endorphins (pleasure hormones) into her blood. These endorphins help her neurons to grow by regulating levels of glucose and insulin. Dopamine – which is a neurotransmitter – is also released from her brainstem and enhances the uptake of glucose, which helps new brain tissue to grow.

Having lots of positive experiences early in life helps create more dopamine receptors in the frontal cortex, which will eventually help your child to evaluate events and adapt to them quickly, to delay gratification and to think about choices of action.

Watch your baby. She uses her huge eyes and overly large pupils as a cunning ploy, which we adults use as well. Across a room a man and woman will unconsciously signal their mutual attraction by flashing their pupils at each other. Your baby uses this trick to let you know she wants you, and as you come closer, her pupils enlarge even more, making you well up with love and the desire to cuddle her.

The upshot? All that time sitting staring into your baby's eyes is actually helping her brain to grow!

Establishing arousal levels

Some psychologists now believe that in the early months of a baby's life, she establishes a 'normal' range of arousal, a particular point which her systems will attempt to maintain, so when things drop below or rise above this normal range of arousal, her regulatory systems go into action to recover this set point. Babies whose mothers are depressed for instance, adjust to low stimulation levels and get used to a lack of positive feelings, which is why it is really important to get help as soon as possible if you suspect you are suffering from post-natal depression.

They also suggest that adults who develop post-traumatic stress disorder (the inability to recover from trauma) may be those whose emotional systems were less robustly built as babies.

This is also a good example of how genes and the environment interact with each other; instructions from our genes ('grow a human brain') depend on environmental factors (affection from other people) to be realized.

The structure of the brain

We can trace our evolutionary history in our individual brains. The inner most part of the brain is our most primitive and something we share with reptiles; it includes the brainstem which is responsible for things we have no control over like breathing, heart rate, digestion and reflexes, but also includes the hypothalamus which is responsible for regulating and maintaining systems and thus influences us unconsciously, making us find water when we are thirsty for instance. Finally there is the amygdala which is responsible for our response to fear – the 'flight or fight' response.

On top of that primitive brain grows the main structure of the brain, what we would recognise from pictures, the cerebrum. This is the brain we share with mammals, but the wrinkly surface which overlies it all, the top few layers of cells, is the cortex and this is unique to human beings. This bit gives us language, reasoning, our ability to do maths or write novels, and also our ability to override our primitive emotional responses. This part of the brain develops last, and sections of it actually develop after birth.

Although these areas of the brain appear separate, they are all linked together and work together at all times. So for example, the primitive part of your brain will register that you are holding something hot, and instinctively get you to pull your hands away, but at the same time your cortex tells you that in fact you're holding a valuable plate, and overrides your primitive responses, thus saving the plate from destruction.

A baby can't exercise this restraint though, and even as a toddler she would drop the hot plate automatically, because her frontal cortex, which is responsible for this type of self-control, only develops over the first few years of life. This makes sense as it can develop in response to what our social world needs. Perhaps some cultures would not need to worry about dropping expensive china for instance. Perhaps in a culture where there is a constant threat to survival, allowing the amygdala full control might be advantageous.

More subtly, think about the difference between the English 'stiff upper lip' and the Italian 'hot blooded emotion'. These two nations share a similar gene pool; it is the upbringing, the culture, that creates different emotional responses, rooted in the brain's frontal cortex. So if you value self-expression in your child, you will allow her free rein with her emotions, and not disapprove of her when she cries or later on as a toddler, when she throws a tantrum. On the other hand, not responding to her as a baby when she cries or tries to interact with you, is more likely to create a child who has no understanding of her emotions – the stiff upper lip, repressed type of adult who lacks emotional intelligence.

Babies therefore need lots of positive social interaction in their formative years in order to develop a social conscience, so they can develop this capacity to override their primitive responses. Lots of communicating and interacting with you strengthens the links between your baby's frontal cortex and her amygdala, so that she too in time will be able to override the amygdala's flight or fight response and develop social control and responsibility.

Can babies exercise self-control?

'Is she a good baby?' seems to be one of the first questions new parents are asked. This begs the question of course, what does 'good' mean for a baby? What the question seems to suggest is that your baby can choose how to behave, that there is some sort of rational process going on in her head, but in fact your baby will not be capable of behaving with intent for a long time, until her frontal cortex develops and can override the purely emotional responses of the more primitive parts of her brain. While this is developing after birth, it doesn't begin to mature until toddlerhood. So babies cannot control their behaviour at all, and even to begin to gain self-control as a toddler they will need lots of positive interactions as a baby.

So when your baby cries she is not trying to manipulate you, she is simply expressing a need and for her to grow as a secure and confident individual, you need to respond to her cries, so she can learn that the world is a good place where she can influence things for the better.

Case study

Jane's baby Abigail is now three weeks old, her partner Allan has gone back to work, and she's on her own at home. She cannot believe how hard it seems to be a mother. She does not seem to get anything done, she is lucky if she manages a shower in the morning and to put a load of washing on. Otherwise much of her time is spent feeding, changing and carrying Abigail around.

What Jane is experiencing is really common, and it is worth remembering that we are a bit odd in our culture, leaving mothers on their own with babies. Other cultures devote at least the first six weeks to nurturing the mother so that she can nurture the baby, and even after these six weeks of 'babymoon', mothers are rarely on their own, but have sisters, aunties and grannies around to help and to share all the domestic chores. Jane will find it is going to take quite some time before she feels on top of everything again.

107
the physical development
of the social baby

08

Summary of this chapter

- Babies are born nine months too early, and mothers need lots of help looking after them. This is one of the reasons we are a sociable species.
- Being born early is actually an advantage as it allows babies to adapt to their social environment.
- The most important parts of your baby's brain actually grows after she is born.
- Babies' brains are incredibly busy, doing most of their growth in the early years, setting up connections which are dependent on their social world.
- Love helps your baby's brain to grow; her social and emotional intelligence is dependent on your responsiveness.

What this means for you and your baby

Every moment you spend interacting with your baby is going to help her develop. She is also not going to be capable of controlling herself emotionally or physically in order to 'behave' as we might understand it. Knowing all this can really help when you feel frazzled by endless crying or sleepless nights!

Understanding how your baby develops what might be called 'emotional intelligence' is useful in realizing that your baby's emotional behaviour is not under her control.

A baby who cries, who demands attention, is not being 'naughty', she is simply expressing how she feels and your role is to help her regulate her emotional states until she's able to do this for herself.

Temperament does affect the amount your baby cries; but the main thing is to respond as far as possible to her needs and to remember that she needs your help. If you respond to her now, she will grow up to be a more cheerful, independent and resourceful child.

09

the first relationship

In this chapter you will learn:
- what psychologists mean by 'attachment'
- how bonding works
- that you can change negative emotional patterns in your family so that your baby will grow up to be an emotionally secure adult.

Emotional security – it's a scary concept. Do babies need their mothers? What happens if you leave your baby with someone else? Arguably no other area of parenting raises more hackles than the issue of who looks after the baby.

We have seen that human beings are very flexible and can adapt to a variety of situations. However, for babies, being able to form strong emotional attachments (bonding) with one or two people is crucial, with long-term effects on mental health if these attachments are disrupted. Why would this be?

- Because a newborn baby is so helpless, a strong attachment must form between baby and carer as soon as possible.
- Such a bond would mean that the baby would know who is looking out for him, so as he becomes mobile he knows where to turn for safety.
- For the grown-up, forming such a strong bond would ensure they want to protect the baby.

This bonding happens for most other animals. For instance, birds do something called 'imprinting', and will follow the first moving thing they see after hatching, even if for some unfortunate babies, that is a human being. A scientist called Karl Lorenz managed to get baby chickens to imprint on him, and even when his chickens met their biological mother, they ignored her and continued to run around after him. In adult life they paid no attention to their own species and instead attempted to mate with humans. Lorenz also showed that there is a very critical time period for imprinting – if baby birds are isolated throughout this critical period they never form attachments to anyone or anything and become socially isolated for the rest of their lives.

Although we are far more flexible and adaptable than birds, the idea of a critical period for bonding, like this imprinting, became popular and it's still not unknown for maternity hospitals to try to enforce a period of 'bonding' according to some arbitrary timetable, despite the fact that several studies in the 1980s found that separating mother and baby after delivery (as was fairly standard practice during this time) had no effect on the strength of later bonds.

Current maternity practices usually involve keeping mother and baby together as far as possible anyway, as 'rooming in' has been demonstrated to enhance the initiation and continuation of breastfeeding, but even so, the idea of a short but critical period for bonding does not seem to be supported by research.

The growth of attachments in babies

Instead, we now know that babies gradually form attachments with one or two people throughout the first year of life, and that babies are most strongly attached to the person who shows them affection and interacts with them, not to those who attend to purely physical needs (although of course this is often the same person).

- **Stage one** – from birth and through the first few months – your baby is interested in people in general, rather than any one person in particular.

  This means that your baby when young is happy to interact with most people, but it is still important that he has continuity in order to progress to the next stage, and it is certainly worth both parents being involved as much as possible at this stage.

- **Stage two** – your baby becomes interested in just a small number of people. This is the beginning of attachment formation and usually happens at around five to seven months of age. For instance, at this age your baby is more likely to smile at particular people and is more easily comforted by them.

  This is the ideal time to let your baby get to know any substitute carers like child-minders and nannies who will be looking after him later on.

- **Stage three** – seven to nine months of age – your baby prefers one particular person (usually his mother). He protests if separated from her, sticks near her if crawling around. He uses his mother as a safe base from which to explore as he becomes mobile. He also begins to show fear of strangers, crying if approached by strange people.

  Your baby will cope better with strangers at this age if they do not approach him suddenly or unexpectedly, but interact with you first, and then gradually include baby in the conversation. At this stage, your baby will be looking at you to see how to react, and if he can see that you are getting along well with someone, he is more likely to accept them.

- **Stage four** – at this stage your child begins to be able to take your needs into account, and may accept being left for short periods. This usually occurs by age three, though some two-year-olds can do this.

It helps if you can be really explicit about what is going to happen; 'I am just going to go to the shops to buy us some lunch and then I will come back and get you. You can stay here and play with the lovely toys instead, and I will be back very soon.' It is better to reassure your child, even if it makes the parting longer and more difficult, than to try and sneak out of the door when he is not looking.

• **Stage five** – lessening of attachment – school-age child. Your child doesn't need to be near you now, but has developed an internal working model of the relationship to sustain him in periods of separation, and is capable of understanding abstract notions such as affection, trust and approval.

Fascinating fact
Bonding happens in the brain.

These stages of emotional development can be seen happening bio-chemically. Between six and 12 months, there is a massive increase in synaptic connections in the prefrontal cortex inside your baby's brain, which is the part of the brain responsible for emotional regulation, so this growth happens just when the attachment bonds are being consolidated. This growth spurt finally peaks in early toddlerhood, or around stage three of attachment formation.

What makes a baby emotionally secure?

Babies are more securely attached if their mothers and fathers respond sensitively to them. In particular, your baby is more likely to be securely attached if you have 'mind-mindedness', which means that you treat your baby as an individual with a mind, so you try to respond to what you think is your baby's state of mind inferred from cues, rather than just responding to your baby's behaviour.

Case study

A good example can be found by watching Shirley, who is an experienced mother as she already has a daughter aged three, trying to calm her six-week-old baby Milo.

She picks Milo up, holds him along her forearms so she is supporting his head in her cupped hands. This means that if he stops crying and opens his eyes, he will be looking straight at her.

She gently moves her arms up and down, rocking him. She alternates this with a swaying of her hips, thus dancing with him from side to side.

As she does this, she is talking to him all the while, in a concerned voice, 'What's the matter, Milo? Are you feeling upset? What's wrong? Is your nappy dirty? Did that horrid noise outside frighten you?' and so on.

Of course Milo cannot understand what she is saying, but he will calm down and then she will continue to interact with him like this.

The point here is that she is treating him as a real person with a mind and is trying to understand why he is upset. The more she does this, the easier it will become for her to figure out what is going on in his head, and the more he will come to see how she cares for him.

Secure attachment

Most babies, especially if their parents respond to their needs, will be emotionally secure children and grow up to be emotionally secure adults. These children, especially when young, want to be close to their mothers, particularly when reunited after a separation. They may or may not be distressed when she goes, but if they are, it's because of her absence, and if they do get distressed, she can comfort them easily when she returns.

While separation anxiety – crying when left, being comforted when you return – might seem to suggest that your baby is insecure, in fact this is the sign of a healthy bond between parent and child, and babies who show this separation anxiety develop into more independent and secure children.

A mother who is sensitive to her baby's cues was probably securely attached to her own parents, and now values her own experiences of being parented, or at least is aware of the value of such experiences. Her baby grows up to become an **autonomous** adult who can recall his own childhood experiences objectively and openly.

Insecure attachments

Some children, however, become what psychologists call insecurely attached, and these insecurities can be passed on from generation to generation, as babies grow up to be parents whose own emotional security influences how they respond to their babies.

In our society right now parents often feel under pressure to get their babies to be independent as soon as possible, and some of these will respond by ignoring or make light of any clinginess or neediness that their baby demonstrates. It's not that the parents don't care; it's just that they don't think the baby's emotional state is particularly important. (Leaving babies to cry it out so they don't get 'spoilt' might be a typical reaction of this parent.)

The problem with this parenting approach is that while on the surface these children may appear calm and independent, and may also have low baseline levels of cortisol, having managed to switch off the stress response, it could be argued that suppressing feelings does not make them go away, but can result in uncontrollable or unpredictable outbursts of emotion.

Sadly these babies sometimes grow up to be bullies at school, some become whiny or clingy children while others, having stopped expecting emotional warmth, act as if they don't care, but will show more distress when under pressure than securely attached children.

In addition, if a mother dismisses her baby's state of mind and is unresponsive to her baby's cues – perhaps because she does not value her own childhood experiences and may not have felt secure herself as a baby – her baby may grow up to become the **dismissive** adult who sees relationships as of little value.

The other type of insecurity which can be perpetuated over generations is when a mother is angry or in some other way bound up in unresolved feelings about her own childhood, and her response to her baby is inconsistent. If parents blow hot and cold emotionally, they can leave the child unsure of what to expect. The baby grows up to become an **enmeshed** adult, preoccupied with dependency on his own parents and still trying to please them.

At the extreme end of this is the mother who has unresolved trauma or loss associated with her childhood (she may have been abused for instance). From the baby's point of view, she is either frightened, frightening, or worse still she may abuse the

child herself. Baby becomes an **unresolved** adult who cannot come to terms with his own experiences. This type of person is most likely to be anti-social, aggressive or psychopathic.

Change is possible

All this sounds terribly frightening, but what it highlights is just how important parental love is for children. And the good news is that nothing is set in stone, change is possible. Children's emotional security can change over time; for instance, a securely-attached child can sometimes change to feel insecurely attached because of major life events affecting his whole family, like his parents separating or having financial difficulties. It can work the other way too; children can change from insecure to secure, usually because their family situation has improved.

There is also evidence that adults can resolve their issues with attachments through counselling or reflection, and can thus break the cycle of insecure attachment by responding in a different way to their babies.

Indeed being aware of the issues that affect you can help; survivors of the Holocaust who were children during that terrible time and lost their parents, grew up, not surprisingly, into *unresolved* adults. However, they did not transmit this type of attachment fully; instead their children had slightly higher unresolved attachment than normal but their grandchildren had no unresolved issues of attachment.

Case study

Vanessa's daughter Natalie is, at six months, a very happy baby and smiles at everyone. Vanessa has noticed that her friend's baby, who is a little older, is very clingy and hates letting his mother out of his sight, even for an instant. Vanessa is wondering what her friend has done to deserve this!

While Vanessa might congratulate herself on helping Natalie through her first few months into being such a cheery baby, it is probable that Natalie too will become very clingy in a couple of months time, as she reaches the stage of separation anxiety. While this may be difficult to cope with at the time, it is perfectly normal and will pass. Vanessa will need to be patient and kind with Natalie until she regains her cheerful friendliness again.

Summary of this chapter

- Emotional security comes from being with parents who are responsive.
- It unfolds gradually over time and does not depend on any small but critical time period.
- Emotionally insecure adults tend to have emotionally-insecure children – but you can break the cycle.

What this means for you and your baby

It's important that you respond to your baby as a person, and to try to understand what is going on for him and act accordingly. It doesn't matter whether you get this right every time, the main thing is that you are trying to help and trying to understand.

Rushing your baby into independence before he is ready is a mistake. It's probably best to follow your baby's lead in this. If he is happy to be left with different people or to play on his own, then take advantage of this, but don't force him if he is unhappy. There is no rule about when your child will be ready for independence as each child varies.

Some people find it hard to cope with dependence in children if they were forced to renounce this themselves. If you are feeling unhappy about responding to your baby's needs, perhaps it is worth really looking at where your feelings are coming from. By doing so you might be breaking a family history of insecure attachment.

Childcare books which insist that all children should behave in the same way, that they have the same needs, need the same responses, should be treated with caution. This is not mind-mindedness. A book which talks about responding to a child's behaviour (whether feeding, sleeping or crying behaviour) with set strategies is not likely to be helpful unless this particular strategy just happened to be the one your baby needed at that particular time! In which case you will probably use that strategy anyway without the book's help.

10

childcare

In this chapter you will learn:
- whether babies always bond with their mother first
- the implications of attachment theory for childcare
- what you should do if you are returning to work.

We saw in the previous chapter that during your baby's first year, she will form a strong emotional bond with adults and that these attachments will be secure or insecure depending on how these adults behave towards her. In today's world, where most mothers return to work within a year of giving birth, how important is it that your baby attaches to just one person?

Can babies bond with lots of people?

If you compare children from disturbed backgrounds who are raised in institutions with children from similar backgrounds who are raised by foster parents, even though neither group does as well at school as children from ordinary backgrounds, the institutional children are far more likely to be inattentive, hyperactive and emotionally disturbed than the fostered children. Children who came from happy families but who grew up in the kibbutz in Israel tell a similar story. These children were raised communally and only saw their parents for an hour or two a day, and they too turned out to be insecurely attached. It seems therefore that babies do need to attach to a small number of people, so institutional care, or care by several people, does not seem to work well for young babies.

> This is the reason that social workers will always try to find foster parents rather than using institutional care for children at risk, and when children are ill, hospitals will encourage parents to visit as often as they can or even to stay in with them.

How many people can your baby bond with? When babies first start to object to being separated, they protest about being parted from one particular person only, but as they get older, typically at about 18 months, they show separation anxiety for more than one person. Also, one third of babies form their strongest or primary attachment to someone other than their mother, be it a grandparent, their father or even an older sibling. Bonds are formed, not with the person who changes the baby's nappies and generally looks after their physical needs, but with the person who interacts and plays with them the most.

Why is this? To understand, we need to think about why your baby is anxious about separation in the first place. Separation anxiety is not about fear of loss of protection, but about the fact that the baby has learnt to communicate with one person in a form that is highly specific to the two of them. She's afraid of a stranger approaching or her mother disappearing because she's only learnt to communicate with that one other person. (See Chapter 15 for more about this early communication.)

As she grows older and her language skills develop, she will become more skilled in communicating with all members of her family, and so she will be happy to be left with these different people. However, she will still be afraid of completely unknown people until her communication skills are mature enough to communicate with the world at large.

Are day nurseries OK?

If babies attach to only one or two people, what then, are the implications for today's society where over 70 per cent of mothers return to work within their baby's first year, and over 95 per cent of fathers work full-time?

Childcare options are partly influenced by government thinking, and it could be argued that the current government seems to favour day nurseries over other arrangements. In Sweden, parents have the choice between extended maternity and paternity leave or day nursery, and they have on the whole opted for the extended leave so that today practically no babies attend day nursery in Sweden. But this is still not a realistic option in the UK, where almost 250,000 children under three years of age currently attend a day nursery. This is a massive increase on previous rates, and to top that, the hours that babies spend in day nurseries has also increased, with some babies there up to ten hours, five days a week.

Unfortunately, what evidence there is does suggest that care of this type for such long periods of time is not the best option for children under three. The National Institute of Child Health and Development (NICHD) has been studying 1,200 children in daycare in the USA over several years and reporting every few years on their findings. In the UK a similar study has been happening at the University of London; EPPE (Effective Provision of Pre-School Education) has been following 3,000 children from babyhood onwards, and Penelope Leach and colleagues have also been doing a longitudinal study of 1,200 children in the UK.

All of this research has come to similar conclusions, namely that day nursery care of more than 20 hours per week for children in their first year of life creates insecure attachments in 43 per cent of babies, whereas for babies who only attend day nursery part time or not at all, only 26 per cent have insecure attachments.

Babies in day nurseries have also been found to have higher levels of cortisol (stress hormones) than babies at home with parents. Even if the baby appears calm and accepting, inside they may be under significant stress.

Having said that, the EPPE study found that for 3–5-year-olds, pre-school experience helps children learn, especially if they are from a disadvantaged background. However, the benefits peak at 20 hours a week and there's no extra benefit in attending nursery full-time. Also, these advantages did not last in the long run unless the child's home environment was particularly lacking. Children who were at home full-time were quickly able to catch up on the intellectual skills once they started school.

How could day nurseries work well for babies?

Babies need one or two adults to interact with, to develop that primary communication – intersubjectivity – which is the root of language, learning and social behaviour (see Chapter 15).

Babies form attachments with people who interact with them. If several people look after a baby for most of her waking hours, there may not be anyone to form these attachments with. Professional care is not the same as intimate care, where games are played over nappy changing, where eye contact conveys emotions and love. Staff cannot show the real affection and love that a parent can, though they can try hard.

Day nurseries *can* be responsive to baby's needs if they designate one member of staff to work with each baby, thus allowing a primary attachment to form, as long as that member of staff has only a small number of babies to look after and is actually interested in forming a relationship with her charges. She would presumably also need to be paid well to motivate her to stay. Unfortunately many day nurseries in the UK, being run as they are, currently as profit-making businesses charging competitive rates, can't always afford to offer this type of care.

Alternatives to day nurseries

Alternatives to day nurseries exist: childminding has been dismissed in the past as low quality babysitting, but in recent years the NCMA (National Childminding Association) has raised the standards of childminding in England and Wales with two quality assurance schemes, one for approved childminding networks (NCMA Children Come First), and one for individual childminders (NCMA Quality First) see **www.ncma.org.uk** (SCMA in Scotland has similar schemes – **www.childminding.org**).

The researcher who looked at cortisol levels in babies in day nurseries also had a look at babies with childminders and found that those who were placed with highly responsive childminders had normal cortisol levels.

So perhaps what matters is the quality of the replacement care and whether the person caring is really paying attention to your child – children at home with parents who are mentally unavailable are no better off than children in full-time day-care; children of alcoholic parents have been found to have high cortisol levels, for instance.

One of the other issues is that lots of childcare early on can make mothers less sensitive to their babies. This might be because the mother has less time to spend with her baby and to get to know her; it could also be that mothers who know that they are to be parted from their babies early due to returning to full-time work, avoid getting too attached, try to keep their babies at an emotional distance, so that the wrench is not so great.

This is completely understandable, but worrying. If you are intending to return to work early, it is important that you focus on your baby during maternity leave and try to forget about the time ahead.

Falling in love with your baby will make returning to work a wrench, but it is far better for her of she has a secure bond with you when you have to part.

Case study

Cathy is enjoying being at home with Daisy far more than she expected, and is now beginning to dread the thought of returning to work. She never imagined before she gave birth that she might want to be a 'stay at home mum'. Her maternity leave seems to be passing so quickly...

It is almost impossible to imagine what being a mother feels like until you actually get there, and this causes a huge dilemma for women like Cathy who were expecting to feel fine about returning to work when their baby is still tiny. Rather than feel guilty about her change of heart, Cathy should try and investigate her options. Does she need to go back to work; could the family cope without her income for a little longer? There are lots of other possibilities too like flexible working hours or working part-time, which it is worth considering.

Summary of this chapter

• Babies form attachments with limited numbers of people, usually those who interact with them.

• The current structure of childcare in the UK is not always conducive to creating emotionally-secure children.

• There are positive alternatives which can work well for babies.

What this means for you and your baby

Does this mean mothers 'should' stay at home and look after their children full-time? Not at all. What it means is that *long* hours over a *long* period of time in day nurseries should be avoided for *very young* children, and this makes sense when you consider what babies need and what day nurseries can offer. However, the best thing for your child is probably for you to:

• investigate the possibility of flexible working patterns for both parents so you can share the childcare.

• check out whether you could draw on extended family or friends where possible to fill in gaps. Perhaps you could swap hours with a trusted friend who has children the same age.

• find quality registered childminders, who you know or trust or who come recommended. If you can find one who is part of the NCMA schemes, even better, as they will have more structured support and training.

• visit any potential childminder when she is working, and see how she interacts with the children in her care. If she welcomes the opportunity of your visit to drop everything and have a good natter, then she is probably not the one for you. Don't be put off if she has rampageous toddlers in her charge; your baby will probably adore the extra stimulation!

- check out a day nursery during working hours (not at a specially arranged open day) and observe how the carers interact with the babies and children. It's easy to be impressed by expensive toys and equipment and ignore the quality of care, especially if you are a new and inexperienced parent. Instead, find out what staff turnover is like and make sure that there will be a designated worker for your baby. Ideally too, you want to meet this designated worker and see how she interacts with your baby.

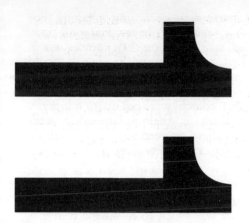

becoming a family

In this chapter you will learn:
- about the effect of having a baby on your relationship
- how fathers interact with their children
- what happens to children after divorce
- how step families and single parent families work.

Traditionally there was a pattern to becoming a family. For previous generations courtship, which may have taken some time, was followed by engagement, marriage, and then couples would begin to have babies. Usually too at this point the woman would stop working and stay at home full-time to bring up the children. Having a baby outside this structure was a matter of deep shame, and most babies born 'outside wedlock' were put up for adoption. Couples who faced difficulties in their relationship were encouraged to work through these or even suppress or ignore them; divorce or separation was a much less acceptable solution.

While there is plenty that was wrong with such a scenario, particularly for women who often felt stifled and disempowered by the division of labour in the traditional nuclear family, as far as the children were concerned, there was much to commend it in that children's physical and mental health, good behaviour and academic achievement all depend on a stable family background.

Nowadays the traditional family structure has changed immensely; the Millenium Cohort Study **www.oneplusone.org.uk** has found that only 60 per cent of people are married when they become parents, 25 per cent are cohabiting, and the other 15 per cent are a disparate group some of whom are separated or divorced, others are closely involved, others are 'just friends.'

Having a baby puts an immense strain on a relationship, so if the couple are still getting to know each other, or are not particularly committed before they have a baby, they are less likely to be together a year after the baby is born (94 per cent of married couples will still be together a year after the baby is born, 75 per cent of cohabiting couples will still be together, but of those who were only 'romantically involved' before the baby arrived, 48 per cent will no longer be together). Many couples cannot cope with consolidating their own relationships at the same time as taking on this new role of parent.

While 18–30 per cent of couples feel their relationship improves after having a baby, for most of us, becoming parents puts a large strain on the relationship.

Relationships under pressure

Why is your relationship under strain when you have a baby?

- Looking after a baby takes a lot of time, which means you have less time for each other.
- You then communicate less with each other.

- When you don't communicate, misunderstandings arise.
- Tiredness and lack of communication means less sex and less intimacy.
- Couples often find themselves forced into traditional divisions of labour and feel resentful about this if this division was not made explicit.
- Post-natal depression (mother or father) can impact on a relationship.
- A 'difficult' baby exacerbates all these problems.

The pressure of combining work and childcare adds to modern parents' burdens, making life a juggling act with every moment accounted for and no time to relax and be together.

Interestingly, the Millennium Cohort Study found that mothers become disenchanted with the relationship during the first year after the baby's birth, while for the father, disenchantment sets in during the second year of the baby's life. However, the effect on the father of feeling dissatisfied with his partner is that he becomes less involved with the baby, and this can generate a negative spiral in that the less involved he is with the baby, the more the mother resents him; he picks up on this and feels even more unhappy with his partner, so he becomes ever more distanced from the baby, and so on.

Even though you will be tired and overworked in your baby's first year, it is really important that you make time for each other, and that you keep the channels of communication open. Make a pact to regularly tell each other how you feel – it's not enough to just talk about mundane things like whose turn it is to load the dishwasher – this is not the sort of communicating you need to do to keep the relationship alive.

Some suggestions:

- Go for a walk together every Saturday afternoon with baby in a sling or pushchair and just talk.
- Get a babysitter once a fortnight and get out of the house for a meal together. Babysitting circles are a good idea, where you take turns with other new parents to babysit. NCT may have a babysitting circle in your area, or you could form one from your antenatal classes. Ring 0870 444 8707 for your local branch.
- Take turns to have a lie in on Sunday morning and recharge your batteries.
- Ask your partner for what you need.
- Don't expect your partner to do everything in the same way you do, but be grateful to each other for the help.

Fathers and children

Fathers' role in looking after children has changed dramatically over recent years. In the 1960s, fathers were discouraged from attending the birth, and those who helped after or during the night were in a minority. Now most fathers attend the birth of their children, most help in the period after, and most get up to help with the baby at night.

Who changes the nappies?

Interestingly, numbers of fathers changing nappies has stayed constant throughout the time: around 40 per cent of fathers in the 1960s never changed nappies and this is still true today, while about 20 per cent of fathers then and now state they 'often' change their baby's nappy. Despite the fact that fathers are more 'hands on' now, mothers still do the majority of basic childcare, while fathers tend to spend their time playing or doing recreational activities with their children.

Difference between mothers and fathers

While men and women are equally capable of bringing up children, they do bring slightly different approaches to parenting, and women will tend to be 'nurturers' – seeking to connect, be intimate with and respond to their children, while men tend to be 'encouragers' – stressing the importance of children's independence and encouraging risk-taking behaviour. While these are both equally valid approaches, problems arise when one parent values their own approach over the other; for instance, emphasizing independence as more important than intimacy may undermine the bonding process, and this ironically can interfere with the child's natural development towards independence, as we saw in Chapter 09.

This is an important point. You and your partner will approach parenting differently, and you both need to value what the other does. Your baby will enjoy the cuddles and fussing and the protectiveness she gets from Mum, but her face will light up when she sees Daddy, and gets ready for the bouncing and throwing and tickling that he provides.

As your children get older, having one parent who is cautious and another who pushes them into trying new things is no bad thing – you will balance each other out. Try to do what feels right for you, and don't be tempted to tell your partner how to parent – both styles will give your baby different things.

Some men find it easier to relate to their children once they begin to speak, as they no longer have to rely on non-verbal cues for understanding. Once their children can communicate, fathers tend to prefer to talk to their children to teach them things, while mothers value talk that is about establishing connections and intimacy.

Having said that, if fathers are given the opportunity and the encouragement to be intimate with their children from an early age, once bonding happens, men interact with their children in a similar way to women, and the more they interact with their offspring, the gentler and kinder they become. Interestingly, a study of 90 non-industrial societies found that the more men were involved in child rearing, the higher the status of women in society.

Fascinating fact
How fathers bond with their babies.

What helps fathers attach to their babies? An experiment in Sweden set out to discover this. People were given identical t-shirts to sniff; one set of t-shirts were newly washed, one set had been worn for a few days by newborn babies, and a third set had been worn for a similar period of time by 2–4-year-old children.

They found that the women could not tell the difference between the worn t-shirts and actually preferred the newly washed ones. However, the men, especially if they were fathers, preferred the t-shirts smelling of a newborn baby.

Analysing the chemical make-up of these t-shirts, the researchers concluded that these smelt of pheromones, and suggested that newborn babies gave out this smell in order to counter any possible aggression from the men. This would tie in with findings that new fathers have lower levels of testosterone, which would tend to make them gentler and more relaxed. (But in case you think this means that mothers are insensitive to their own babies' smell, have a look at Chapter 03.)

Single parent families

When fathers become single parents, they tend to change their parenting styles so they become more like mothers. They form stronger attachments with their children, play less rough and tumble, and instead get more involved in intellectual and creative activities. It may be true that some single fathers find discipline easier than mothers, but others find it harder – single fathers are statistically more likely to batter their children. Many single parent families – male and female – find an egalitarian style of parenting often works well.

Single parent families are not a recent phenomenon, but factors conspire to make their job today far harder than before.

Only a couple of generations ago, most people lived in an extended family, with grandparents, aunts and uncles all living nearby and part of the day-to-day household. It's far less usual to live close to any relatives today. All parents can feel isolated at home with children, but this feeling can be much worse if there is no one with whom to share worries and concerns.

Apart from isolation, poverty is the other burden single parents face. An American study showed that children without fathers at home were five times more likely to be poor, while in the UK most of the children living 'below the poverty line' are in lone parent households. The cost of living is geared to dual income households – reflected in house prices, rents, holidays, even food. How depressing that bulk purchases of food can save you money, while small portions cost more!

The effect on children of divorce

While children with behaviour problems are more likely to come from a non-traditional family structure, it's the stress within the family that creates insecure attachments, not the make-up of the family itself. Conflict between parents is stressful for children, whatever the outcome. If parents stay together and fight this is stressful for children; if they separate and divorce it is also stressful. So it is not divorce or separation that is problematic, but the conflict itself.

Divorce affects children in different ways depending on their age

Pre-school children are upset but not necessarily able to understand; middle childhood children understand but are less able to let go – they fantasize about parents getting back together; while teenagers tend to react with shame or anger, or by siding with one parent over the other.

Many children are at risk of moderate to severe depression even five years or more after the separation. The best outcomes are where children are able to develop good relationships with both parents and where conflict has stopped.

Children of divorced parents often seem more independent, and while mothers and daughters seem to recover and get along OK, mothers and sons tend to have more conflict. In fact, the effect of divorce on boys seems to be more profound. They tend to continue to have behaviour problems, growing up to be more anti-social and non-compliant than boys from intact families. Boys who grow up in a stressful environment are more likely to become fathers themselves at an early age and probably not live with their children.

Intellectually too there is an effect. If a father is very involved with his children, then his sons have better verbal skills than boys with uninvolved fathers, and his daughters will have higher social and cognitive skills than girls with uninvolved fathers.

But both boys and girls score higher on achievement tests if they have one full-time parent who spends a considerable amount of time interacting with them (which may be less possible in a single parent family, especially if that parent has to work).

Entrance exam scores at American universities show that regardless of the socio-economic status of the family, students' scores are 'dramatically lower' from families with an absent father; indeed there is also evidence that children in the States without fathers at home are twice as likely to drop out of school.

Having said that, recent studies of children raised only by their mothers found that they interacted *more* with their mother than children living in two parent families, and that they had more secure attachments, but they had lower self-esteem.

What is important is that you make sure you have plenty of time for your children if you are raising them by yourself. Emotional security is more important than financial security as far as your baby is concerned, so it may be that for a few years you need to really cut back on things, and only return to full-time work when your baby reaches school age.

Fascinating fact
Single parent families are not a new phenomenon!

Interestingly, marital breakdown rates are no worse today than they have been throughout history.

In pre-industrial Britain and throughout the nineteenth century, one in three marriages ended prematurely – similar to today's rates, but then marriages often ended because of death – 8 per cent of mothers died in childbirth for instance, while others ended through formal separation (divorce was not legalized in England and Wales until 1957).

Effects on grandparents

One of the more recent issues in family breakdown is for grandparents and the loss of access after divorce. A study in the UK found grandparents suffering chronic grief, mental health problems and even post-traumatic stress after being deprived of access to grandchildren.

Stepfamilies

Most new parents start out as part of a couple. If relationships break down, many of the resulting lone parents do not want to remain single forever either, and most single parent families do not remain so for long – remarriage is common, so we also need to look at the effects on children of having step-parents. Evidence suggests that a stepfather seems to improve matters for sons, but made things worse for daughters, so while sons need more help when a family breaks down, daughters need that help when families are re-created.

Gay families

What is the effect on children of being raised by two parents of the same sex? Research suggests that the gender identity and sexual preferences of children raised in gay families are no different from children raised in heterosexual families. However, they potentially have more problems with friendships, probably through being teased about having an unconventional set-up at home. You can be aware of this and make sure the channels of communication stay open; the first thing to do is to give your child a positive vocabulary to describe their home set-up.

Whatever your family structure looks like today, it may well be different tomorrow. Families now are more fluid and changeable than ever before. Single parent families are unlikely to remain single for long – on average about three and a half years. Ironically, when we consider how much negative press single parent families are given, it seems that some children may suffer more on remarriage. They often feel threatened by this interloper, who competes for their parent's attention. If stepbrothers and stepsisters are part of the package it can be even more alarming. Parents need to handle new family relationships extremely carefully, and seek support and advice where possible.

Case study

Rebecca is on her own with Alice as her partner walked out when she was pregnant. She feels she is fairly well set up; her mother lives nearby and is keen to help out, and will look after Alice when Rebecca returns to work part-time. Rebecca though, is a bit worried about the effect on Alice of having no father figure around.

It sounds as if Rebecca has a good set-up here, and Alice should do just fine. A lack of a father figure might seem a problem, but later on Rebecca might be able to find a male friend or relative who is willing to take on this role in a small way. If Rebecca forms a relationship with someone else, she will need to handle this carefully and sensitively, and introduce any new partner slowly but positively.

Summary of this chapter

- Family structures are more varied now than they have ever been.
- Having a baby puts a strain on all relationships, but particularly on the non-traditional set-ups.
- Men and women parent in different ways, both equally important.
- Family discord affects children whether or not it ends in separation or divorce.
- Boys are more affected by family stress than girls.

What this means for you and your baby

If you are a single parent, isolation can be a problem, so try to develop your own 'extended family'. Parent and toddler groups, babysitting circles etc. are obvious sources of friendship and support, but cultivate your neighbours too. Perhaps an elderly couple are feeling equally isolated from their own family and would love to become involved with yours! Ask your health visitor for resources, contacts and ideas. Gingerbread also run local support groups for single parents (**www.gingerbread.org.uk**).

Poverty can also be an issue; make sure you are getting *all* the benefits you are entitled to. Contact your nearest citizens advice bureau **www.citizensadvice.org.uk**, or Gingerbread **www.gingerbread.org.uk**, or the national council for one parent families **www.oneparentfamilies.org.uk**. Keep an eye out for thrift and nearly-new shops. E-bay and garage sales are a boon to the cash strapped parent.

New relationships – incredibly difficult to get this right. New families can be painful and stressful for children, but ultimately, if they work, they can function much as extended families did in the past. Expect fireworks in the meantime, whatever age your children. It may help to contact Parentline Plus on 0808 800 2222 or the Stepfamily Helpline Scotland on 0845 1228655.

12

your baby's position in the family

In this chapter you will learn:
- whether birth order affects personality
- how sibling rivalry impacts on children.

Eighty per cent of us have siblings usually only a few years older or younger than ourselves. Some siblings get on well and are a great source of companionship and support, while others fight almost continually. What is clear is that the relationship is rarely, if ever, one of indifference.

Sibling relationships

Having a sibling certainly makes children more aware of others in that children who have siblings have a more complex understanding of social relationships and of other people's points of view. Some children can be very tolerant of younger siblings, others can be at best ambivalent, at worst hostile, and these reactions happen in all societies throughout the world.

Getting the relationship off to a good start is important; a study showed that children who were aged 1–3 years when their younger sibling was born and who showed friendly interest and concern for the new baby in the first three weeks of her life, were more likely to show concern if their sibling was hurt or distressed at a follow-up six years later.

On the other hand, babies who grow up with an unfriendly or hostile sibling are more likely to be anxious, depressed or aggressive as adolescents. Also, if children think that their sibling receives more attention and affection, they are more likely to be aggressive or difficult.

What is certainly true is that having a sibling creates strong emotions, whether love, hate or jealousy (or a mixture of all of these). When they are younger, siblings are useful in that they can use each other to test out relationships, to experiment with making friends for instance. In the process they may swing between affection and hatred, but what seems to make a big difference is if their parents talk to them about these feelings and explain their actions in these terms. This explaining really helps create a positive emotional relationship between siblings.

Case study

As an example, three-year-old Tom has just snatched a brick from his brother Ben, six months, who responds by bursting into tears. Their mother Elaine could just tell Tom off, but the best response is to tell Tom that his actions were wrong – unacceptable – then to point out the consequences of his actions and ask him to think about how Ben feels about what he did.

'That was not a nice thing to do, Tom, you must not snatch toys from Ben. Look, Ben is crying now. What do you think he is feeling? How would you feel if someone snatched something from you?'

If Tom responds well to this – identifies for himself that Ben feels upset for instance and that he (Tom) would also feel upset in that situation, then she can ask him to give the brick back and praise him for his nice behaviour. However, this is quite a difficult thing for Tom to do, so it is also important not to push the point if he does not respond positively this time; over time he will develop this empathy if Elaine continues to be explicit in this way.

Fascinating fact
The natural age gap.

While the four-plus age gap is less common in our society, it is probably what our ancestors experienced. Anthropologists reckon that for most of the human race, children would be spaced four to five years apart through the contraceptive effect of normal long-term breastfeeding.

Effects of birth order

It's a fascinating idea that your personality, intelligence and even career choices might be influenced by the order in which you were born into your family. Alfred Adler (1870–1937), an Austrian psychiatrist and contemporary of Sigmund Freud and Gustav Jung, was probably the first person to publish a theory of personality formation which included birth-order dynamics, but the idea had already been around for centuries.

The important thing to note is that while birth order definitely seems to influence us, other factors are often far more important. Your children will, for instance, behave differently away from the family. Providing your child with a stable family background is far more important, and the overall effect of birth order will also partly be down to how you act towards your children. You may consciously choose to act differently, to minimize the effects of birth order.

Also, you may not *know* that your baby is going to be the youngest, or an only-child or whatever. You might intend to have more children and not succeed or you may accidentally have another child.

Most families these days are fairly small, and so some of the effects noticed in previous generations will no longer apply. When Adler was writing, large families would have been the norm. Spacing is important too; if there is a gap of five or more years between children, it will be as if you have started a second family, so the next new baby will have the characteristics of first-born children. This is probably because their older sibling is more adult-like than child-like. The sex of the child is important as well; a girl born after several boys may be treated as more 'special' for instance.

Having said that, generally the following effects of birth order have been identified:

First-born children (with younger siblings born within five years)

First-borns tend to be more conscientious, more socially dominant, less agreeable and less open to new ideas than later-borns, and this seems to be true in societies throughout the world.

First-born children are often the highest achievers in their family, even if their IQ is the same as later-born children (though usually it is an average of 3.5 points higher). However, they may also feel more anxious and insecure. Later in life they may become authoritarian or strict.

Why is this? Your first-born child initially only interacts with adults and therefore gets more intellectual stimulation than her siblings. However, when her younger sibling is born she may feel unloved, especially if she feels that she has lost out to the new baby. So she may become attention seeking, and look for respect, admiration and approval instead of this lost love.

A first-born often grows up being afraid of losing the top position again, and this makes them more averse to risk. However, sometimes younger siblings idolize the first-born, which must mitigate the effects somewhat.

Parents will often use the oldest child as an additional pair of hands, so first-borns can feel a higher sense of responsibility, may feel less carefree than later-born children. Some parents feel very protective and indulgent towards their first-born child, but other parents can be harsher and set higher standards for the first-born than they do for later children.

And another thing... First-born children are more likely to be disturbing their parents at night beyond three months than later-born children!

Middle child (if surrounded by siblings with less than a five year gap either side)

Traditionally this is seen as a difficult position: initially these children have to share their parents' attention with an older sibling, and when a younger sibling arrives, there is even more competition for even less parental time.

Common characteristics of a middle child can be: skilled mediator, avoids conflict, independent, strong orientation to peer group with lots of friends.

Why is this? Because they need to be fairly skilled to get attention, they develop good social skills. Often they also develop unusual talents, as if they are looking for a way to stand out. Some become quite musical, others become entrepreneurs. Some middle children may become rebellious or non-conformist. It's as if they are spurred on to compete, but knowing the task is pretty impossible, they drop out.

According to Adler, the middle child may have an even-temper and a take it or leave it attitude, feeling compelled to find peace within the family. A favourite phrase of your middle child might be, 'it's not fair!' and these children can become very sensitive to injustice.

And another thing... Middle children have the fewest pictures of themselves on their own in the family album. They are also least likely to be religious.

Youngest child (with sibling no older than five years)

The youngest child is often treated as a baby for longer than the other siblings, and may be indulged or pampered (which according to Adler, is one of the worst things a parent can do, leading to dependence, selfishness and irresponsibility when they are adult. However, it is worth remembering that Adler was a Victorian, and generous displays of affection were not really approved of in that time!).

You may be more relaxed with your youngest baby; you know what you are doing now, and being relaxed, you will probably put less pressure on this child. The youngest also benefits from living in a child-friendly environment, having older siblings to learn from as well as adults. Thus youngest children tend to be emotionally secure, friendly and extroverted. They appear charming, but can also be seen as manipulative. They are less likely to be outstanding at school, despite IQ, perhaps because there is less pressure on them to perform.

Only-children

The only-child is similar in some ways to the first-born, and they start life the same way, but the only-child never has the challenge of adapting to siblings. They may be more adult in their behaviour, but may also be more self-centred and impatient. According to Adler, if they have been over-indulged, they become spoiled and never learn to wait for what they want. However, it is also arguable that they develop self-sufficiency and are happy being alone.

Only-children, like first-borns tend to be more conscientious, more socially dominant, less agreeable, and less open to new ideas. However, only-children do not seem to be any less sociable. It also seems to be the case that only-children are high achievers and have above average IQ scores, though interestingly, not as high as first-borns; typically two or three points lower than an oldest child with one or two younger siblings.

This seems to contradict the idea that first-borns or only-children are benefiting from extra parental attention. If this were true then only-children would be more intelligent than first-borns. Instead it looks as if first-borns benefit from the extra stimulation involved in teaching their younger siblings.

Case study

Gary and Angela are really happy to be parents at last after many years of waiting, but suspect that Josh will always be an only child. Cousins and relatives live some distance away so they are worried about Josh being on his own.

All the research suggests that only-children turn out just fine. Gary and Angela will need to make more effort, let Josh mix with other children at playgroups and the like, and may have to give Josh a bit of coaching in how to interact with other children, but there are so many opportunities out there for mixing with others, they need not worry.

Summary of this chapter

- It is important to encourage positive relationships between siblings right from the start.
- Birth order has an effect on personality, though other factors are also influential. You can also mitigate these effects.

What this means for you and your baby

It is worth being aware of the effects of birth order and making an attempt to minimize the more negative ones. For instance, try to be lenient and affectionate with the first-born, give your middle child plenty of time on his own, and don't always indulge the youngest!

Try to encourage a positive relationship between your children, especially in the first few weeks after any new baby is born. It's important that you take time to talk to your children about the effects of their behaviour. It can be useful to encourage them to put themselves in other people's shoes. 'How do you think your brother might feel when you do that?', for instance.

13

learning to behave

In this chapter you will learn:
- whether children are born with particular temperaments
- how your style of parenting affects your child's behaviour
- how you might change your parenting style as your baby grows into a toddler.

Parents are often surprised to discover that their baby has a definite personality. Are babies born with particular temperaments, or do they acquire them? And how far can we influence children to turn out in particular ways? This chapter will look at these questions.

Temperament

It seems that it's possible to predict temperament even before birth; babies who were more active than average in the womb, are often described by their mothers as more difficult, unpredictable, unadaptable and active once born. This might suggest that your baby is born with a particular temperament; however, it's also probable that he would be affected by how his mother feels about his behaviour and how she responds to him. Interestingly too, boys tend to be fussier than girls at first; newborn boys will tend to startle more easily and be harder to console than girls.

Babies seem from birth to have particular ways of behaving, and parents often refer to them as 'easy' or 'difficult': easy meaning a baby who is able to soothe himself, who seems to have a sunny disposition, is prepared to sleep alone and who does not need much attention, while the difficult baby cries a lot, needs lots of contact, prefers sleeping with his parents, and appears emotionally quite volatile.

Of course we are viewing this through the Western lens which sees early independence as a 'good' thing, and a baby who needs a lot of attention from his parents as 'difficult'. These ideas of what is normal and what is not normal must affect how we parent: if certain behaviour is socially acceptable then there is less pressure on us as parents to feel there is something 'wrong' with our babies.

Independence is highly prized in babies: babies who can self-soothe, who do not 'demand' attention from their parents, who can 'cope' with separation are valued. A mother who picks up on these values and therefore views her baby's dependence as a negative thing, perhaps feeling that it's not OK to respond to her baby's needs for closeness, will certainly affect her baby's security of attachment as we have seen, and may be more broadly influencing her baby's temperament.

Parental responsiveness and temperament

Temperamentally difficult babies are more of a challenge for parents, and seem to be more at risk of later behaviour problems, but if parents are able to respond in a way that suits the baby, outcomes are more positive. For instance, if parents pick up their baby when he cries, in 88 per cent of cases, the baby will stop crying, which is very rewarding. Depressed mothers on the other hand, tend to be less responsive to their babies, and this affects their baby's ability to respond positively to events.

> In one experiment, mothers were randomly assigned to three groups. The first were given a soft baby sling, the second, a plastic baby seat, while the third (control) group were given nothing. When the babies were 13 months old the quality of attachment between mother and baby was assessed blindly (meaning that the researcher assessing this did not know which group the mother and baby belonged to). The research found that the babies who were in soft carriers were more emotionally secure than those in the other two groups, and they cried less.

Fascinating research findings
Responding to babies does not 'spoil' them.

Researchers in Holland worked with over 100 babies over a period of four years, in families where mothers might not normally be responsive to their babies' cries, often from deprived backgrounds.

In some families, experimenters taught the mothers to respond to the babies' cries – the rest were 'control' families. The researchers found that in families where mothers were more responsive, the babies actually cried less.

Babies who discover their dependence and neediness is not welcome, learn to hide their feelings or even to believe they should not have feelings (the traditional English stiff upper lip). These children may then grow into people who have difficulty in recognizing their own feelings – how can you identify your own feelings if you have not had these valued or named?

It is particularly important to name feelings, especially for boys. When your baby starts to acquire a vocabulary, you will respond to what he seems to be interested in, so you will need to make a conscious effort to name things which are less interesting and to comment on and make explicit, social relationships. This is all part of helping your child to have 'emotional intelligence'.

Parenting styles change over time

Parenting styles are also, in part, culturally determined with particular styles coming in and out of fashion.

At the turn of the twentieth century, it was very clear how children should behave – they were to be seen and not heard; and it was equally clear what to do if they didn't – 'spare the rod and spoil the child'. Victorian children needed taming by force and fear.

As the century progressed, physical violence eased, but children were still treated roughly – spanking, and leaving them to cry was seen as 'character building'.

However, by the 1970s and 1980s ideas had changed completely, and children were brought up in a culture where feelings were paramount. Parents were to be child-centred, and smacking was no longer seen as acceptable.

In the 1990s the pendulum began to swing back, and now the current best-sellers are very much about making children adapt to arbitrary routines, not responding to baby's cues but trying to mould baby's behaviour to fit the clock.

It's not surprising these types of books are now popular; in most households both parents work, and several have a single parent. Little backup is available from extended families due to social mobility – the end result is that tired parents are struggling to look after their children, often without any clear idea of what works best. However, as we saw in Chapter 09, you need to respond to your baby as a person, to have mind-mindedness, and trying to ignore your baby's needs and fit him into a timetable or routine according to a book, is likely to create a child who is insecure and who grows up to be an adult who does not value relationships.

Styles of parenting – looking to the future

While it is important that you respond to your baby, what of over indulgence? Can you spoil your baby as he grows older, and how do you get toddlers and older children to behave so they will become acceptable members of society? It is worth thinking now about how you want to parent your baby when he moves into toddlerhood and beyond.

One of the problems of studying the effects of parenting styles is actually to agree on a working definition and then to study the effects of this on children. From a psychological point of view, broadly speaking we could think of parents as being *authoritarian* – having strict ideas about discipline and behaviour which are non-negotiable; *authoritative* – having ideas about discipline and behaviour which they are willing to explain and discuss with their children and perhaps adapt; *permissive* – parents with relaxed ideas about behaviour and discipline. There is another aspect to this, which is how demanding the parents are. For instance, a parent could appear permissive simply because they are not interested, and this is entirely different from a parent who has chosen to be permissive and is thinking about this. So if you put these together, you can see a four-way categorization:

	Responsive	Unresponsive
Demanding	Authoritative	Authoritarian
Undemanding	Permissive	Uninvolved

So what does research show? One study of 122 school-age children observed parents at home to categorize parenting styles, and got ratings from their classmates and teachers at school. The study found that *authoritative* parents have popular, sociable children, whereas *authoritarian* parents tend to have rejected children.

Another much bigger study (6,400 children), which relied however on parents answering a questionnaire to rate parenting styles, found that *authoritative* parenting lead to better school performance. What was particularly interesting was that if parents were very involved in schoolwork, this was *helpful* for authoritatively parented children, but *unhelpful* for authoritarian parented children. Perhaps the latter were overly critical which lead to loss of confidence and opting out. Interestingly there is no research on the effect of permissive parenting on children's attainment, though we know that lack of involvement is not helpful for children in general.

At this stage in your baby's life, i.e. during his first year, you don't really need to worry about discipline as what is important is providing a loving and socially stimulating environment for your baby. However, as you look to the future, it is worth thinking now about how you will be with your baby as he reaches his toddler years, and it seems that authoritative parenting is the most useful for a happy, healthy and likeable toddler. This will mean:

- setting firm boundaries and sticking to them. However, it also means being explicit about this – explaining why something is wrong rather than just imposing your will on your children
- having consequences for misbehaviour
- having lots of rewards for good behaviour
- providing consistent and loving parenting.

To set firm boundaries, it is useful to start thinking now about what will be important to you, and what will be less important, and how you want to respond to different things. You cannot react in the same way if your child runs into the road, swears at granny, chews with his mouth open, and accidentally drops something. Some things will be no and will always be no, and there must be consequences for doing them, while others will be negotiable.

What you need to parent

There is a lot of talk of teaching parenting skills in the current political climate; what resources do people actually need to parent well? One model suggests that three things influence the ability to parent:

- Personal psychological resources.
- Sources of support.
- Characteristics of the child.

Some interventions have focused on improving this first aspect, the personal psychological resources, in particular trying to improve parental sensitivity and thus affect the child's attachment. Others have worked on the second aspect, giving parents increased support through health visitors, education and psychotherapy.

These studies have found that it is possible to increase maternal sensitivity to the child, but harder to improve attachment security, mostly because interventions were aimed at changing *behaviour* rather than the deeper attitudes. (If you remember from Chapter 09 it is mind-mindedness, i.e. responding to the baby's perceived state of mind rather than responding to behaviour, which affects attachment.)

Helping parents with difficult children, the third strand above, continues to be debated. Part of the problem is back to the 'nature versus nurture' argument – are difficult children difficult because they have inherited their behaviour through genetics or are they difficult as a result of the way their parents behave? Then of course we need to realize that the children contribute to the environment in which they are raised: parents' behaviour is influenced by how their children behave. There is also some debate about whether parents or school have the greater influence on older children.

Case study

Fiona and Bob are amazed at the contrast between their two children. Henry, their oldest, was a very fretful baby, needing to be held and carried all the time, though he is now a very robust and cheerful toddler, while on the other hand their new baby Thomas is calm and content, and seems to like nothing better than sitting in his baby chair watching Henry rushing around.

Children do have different temperaments, which are often nothing to do with their parents. Fiona and Bob should congratulate themselves on helping Henry to grow into this robust and cheerful toddler. It is not surprising in some ways that Thomas is calm and content as he has plenty of stimulation from his brother and does not need extra input from his parents. Long may this happy situation continue!

Summary of this chapter

- Children do seem to be born with particular temperaments, but parental response is also important.
- Society may well have an influence on temperament too, insofar as judgements are made about how parents behave with their children, and some parents may end up feeling unable to respond to their babies as they would like.
- Children respond best to firm but fair authoritative parents.

What this means for you and your baby

While it is best to respond to your baby's needs, as they grow into toddlers it will become obvious that they start to need some boundaries. The best style of parenting is 'authoritative' – setting boundaries, which you are willing to explain and on occasions, negotiate.

part

two
intellectual
development

14

how babies learn

In this chapter you will learn:
- how your baby's brain grows
- how babies build up a body of knowledge
- what your baby already knows about the world at birth
- why interacting with your baby is important.

Four weeks after your baby was conceived, her brain already had a recognizable shape. From this point on her brain cells (neurons) multiplied at the amazing rate of 250,000 per minute, and by the time she was born, all these neurons were in place, about 100 billion of them, only a fraction of which she will actually use in her lifetime. But this is not the most amazing thing about her brain, what really counts are the connections between these neurons: the synapses. By adulthood there will be a quadrillion (a thousand trillion) of these, and it is estimated that in her first two years of life, your baby will grow 1.8 million new synapses *per second!*

Although your baby's brain continues to grow in size once she's born, she does not produce any more neurons; instead it is the connections between these cells that multiply and grow, becoming stronger and more conspicuous with repeated use as electrical signals travel along them at up to 250 mph. As these connections grow they push the main bodies of the neurons further apart, while connections that are not used are eventually pruned. In fact, it sounds quite frightening to consider that children lose about 20 billion synapses *per day* between early childhood and adolescence. This radical pruning means that:

- your child's mental processes become more efficient as she gets older; but
- she will also become less flexible and creative, i.e. less suggestible.

Fine tuning the brain

Here we can see that unfolding of genetic potential within an environment we talked about right back in the introduction of the book. The brain has a genetic tendency to develop in certain ways, but the 'use it or lose it' principle allows some flexibility. Genes make neurons grow and send the synapses in the right general direction, but experience connects them up as and when they are used. By producing too many, the brain forces them to compete so that only the most useful ones are used.

Italian doctors were puzzled by the case of a six-year-old boy who was blind in one eye, as they could find no physical reason for his blindness. On talking to his parents they discovered that as a baby he'd had a minor eye infection and so his eye was bandaged. Unfortunately the eye had been covered during a critical period of brain growth, and the neurons responsible for the unbandaged eye had invaded and colonized the part of the visual cortex meant to be responsible for the occluded eye, so by the time it was unbandaged, the connections for the infected eye had nowhere to go.

The advantage of having flexibility in wiring up the brain

Allowing the brain to wire up like this, with areas only becoming specialized through time, protects your baby, so that if part of her brain becomes damaged other areas can take over, or if she is born with one of her senses damaged, the brain can compensate by creating more connections with other organs. So children who are born profoundly deaf use the part of the brain that would normally become the auditory cortex to process visual information instead.

We can also fine tune our brains to suit our environment. If kittens are reared in an environment where their heads are held in such a way that they can only see vertical stripes, then the neurons responsible for sight become far more sensitive to the vertical and very insensitive to the horizontal, in fact they can barely see horizontal lines at all. While this experimental situation produces extreme results, it seems to be true for human beings too. Those of us who are raised in houses or flats (so called 'carpentered' environments) tend to be better at spotting horizontal and vertical orientations than oblique or diagonal, whereas Canadian Indian babies who are raised in teepees are much better at seeing oblique orientations.

Another good reason for this 'plasticity' in wiring is that it allows your baby's head to grow. The retina at the back of our eye is connected to our visual cortex at the back of our brain by a series of neural staging posts. During the first years of life the eye and the brain both grow at different rates so the connections have continually to be broken and remade. So that your baby can continue to see the world, this breaking and remaking must be orderly and relatively resistant to change; what we call specificity. However, the fine detail of the wiring is subtly shaped by early experience – this is plasticity.

A similar flexibility in wiring can be seen with language development: until they are about six years of age children process grammar in both hemispheres, but after that, the processing happens just in the left hemisphere, yet young children who have had their entire left hemisphere removed for medical reasons have developed normal language skills, so they must have adapted the wiring of their brains to compensate.

Scientists explain it like this: imagine that your baby's development unfolding is like a ball rolling down a mountain. Her genes are like gravity, pulling her downwards, but on the way the ball hits lots of obstacles in the environment, making her adapt and change direction. The further down the hill she goes though, the less possibility there is of stopping or even going back up the hill and starting again down the other side.

The growth of an individual

Connections are formed with experience, and as each baby's experience is unique, each brain is also unique. So even though your baby may inherit a combination of her parents' genes, perhaps getting your short sight and your partner's curly hair, who she will ultimately become is a unique person, shaped as her genetic potential is unfolded in the particular environment of her family, her home, her town, country, school and so on.

How your baby interprets what she sees

In order for your baby to accumulate knowledge, wisdom, intelligence – call it what you will – she needs experience, and until she gets moving this will initially involve looking at the world. But how does your baby even begin to make sense of what she sees?

When you look around the world, you are not just seeing, you are interpreting what you see as well. Light waves reach the retina at the back of your eye and this information is transmitted to the visual cortex in your brain where you make sense of it; you 'perceive' it. It is your brain which decides that the small object you are looking at is a car, and simultaneously decides whether it is a big car seen from far away or a toy car seen close up (both of which create the same image on your retina). But how does your baby's brain even begin to work all this out?

Newborn babies cannot see as well as adults; they lack the ability to see detail, they cannot easily track moving objects with their eyes but do this fairly jerkily, and they are not good at scanning objects (casting their eyes over the inside of an object). They are, however, drawn to notice two things:

• Movement
• Strong contrast.

Focusing on contrast means that your baby will pay attention to the boundaries or edges of objects, which is where contrast is strongest. (This is why the camouflage principle works: the deep lines inside the camouflage blur the boundary of the animal.) It is also useful to focus on the outside of objects if you cannot scan them effectively. Movement helps your baby recognize where things begin and end, because as one object moves it obscures other objects, and so the boundaries between different things become more defined. So your baby's early experiences will be about working out where one thing begins and another ends – a reasonable start in a world where nothing is known.

However, the other thing that newborn babies are particularly drawn to look at is the human face.

What is it about the face that attracts babies?

We know that newborn babies can recognize their own mothers' faces within a few days, but in fact what they are paying attention to are those same two things – the boundaries of the face, and the movements it makes. So your baby recognizes you, separating you out from your surroundings, by noticing what your hair looks like. If a mother wears a scarf over her hair, her newborn baby will not necessarily recognize her. In addition, paying attention to the movement of the face means that your baby can notice and respond to your facial expressions. This is enough to get her going, and with time she can respond to more detail. Thus:

- Newborn babies only prefer faces over other objects if they are moving.
- At two months, babies prefer faces, moving or static, to any other object.
- At three months they will look more at static faces than other complicated patterns.

So babies are born ready to attend to moving faces first and foremost, and then having honed in on faces, they gradually over time begin to identify different faces so that as they get older a different processing system takes over allowing them to recognize particular faces, which perhaps cannot kick in until the baby's attention span increases. We know that by six months of age, babies recognize faces using several areas of their brain in both hemispheres, but by 12 months the face processing circuits have become far more specialized and are localized in the right hemisphere.

Fascinating fact
Babies are born to be multi-cultural!

Interestingly, as your baby becomes better at distinguishing different faces, she will also lose the flexibility she had before.

Experimenters examined how well six-month-old babies, nine-month-old babies and adults could discriminate between different human and monkey faces and found that six-month-old babies could recognize all the monkeys' faces and all the people's faces as different; the nine-month-old babies and the adults could recognize all the people as different but saw all the monkeys as the same.

What is happening is that babies are born potentially able to recognize all faces, but with experience their neural networks prune down this ability, focusing on being able to distinguish between the types of faces they will generally encounter the most. This explains the seemingly xenophobic reaction of some people on first meeting different races, 'they all look the same'. In fact, without the experience of seeing many different races through living in a multicultural society, this is probably true.

Building up a body of knowledge

Throughout your baby's early years, everything she experiences will activate different groups of neurons simultaneously, and as patterns are repeated and strengthened so she slowly begins to categorize her experiences, accumulate memories and, for her, life slowly becomes predictable.

So when she sees a mouth open wide she expects to hear 'aaah'. When she sees you approaching, smiling with your arms out, she expects to feel the sensation of being picked up. If her predictions are incorrect, she will be unhappy. By two weeks old, babies expect to hear their mother's voice coming out of her mouth, and as experiments have shown, they get upset if the voice comes from the wrong place – the side of her head for instance, or if a stranger's voice comes out of their mother's mouth.

How babies learn about the world

The best way to understand how your baby learns about the world is to imagine that she develops hypotheses about the way the world works, and then uses her experience to confirm or reject, adapt or modify these hypotheses as appropriate, or to translate this into brain functioning. As experience repeats, it strengthens the neural connections in her brain, so that she knows that such and such an event is linked to something else, with some connections being stronger than others for experiences which are very familiar.

For instance your baby might figure out, 'when Mum puts my coat on and straps me in this chair, it means that in a short time we are going to be swimming'. Of course she does not express her hypothesis in words like that, but this is the best way of understanding what is going on in her head, and that is roughly the mental process we would go through ourselves too.

If you go swimming regularly, and each time it involves putting on her coat and strapping her in her car seat, eventually you will see her getting excited as you are getting ready.

But imagine one day, instead of ending up at the swimming pool, the same sequence of events takes her to the doctor where she is given an injection. She may then modify the hypothesis, so that it now reads, 'when Mum puts my coat on and straps me in this chair, it means that in a short time we are going to get in the car, and then we will either go swimming or something horrible will happen'. And thus she has modified her hypothesis, and will be able to subtly change it as more and more events occur after this sequence of putting on her coat etc.

Babies start off with experiences being very immediate and physical so they are very much in the here and now, but through time they develop more abstract internal representations of the world, and these they also modify with experience by this process of hypothesis testing. An example of an internal representation is that you have one of your baby – you can think about, imagine and plan scenarios involving her without her actually having to be present.

- So when your baby starts to speak, she will talk about things in the here and now, naming objects she can see for instance, and it will be some time before she can talk about things in abstract, i.e. talking about things that happened in the past or are going to happen in the future.

- As we saw in Chapter 09, attachment or bonding evolves so that eventually your baby will be happy to imagine an abstract representation of you rather than having to have you there in reality.

Babies are driven to learn, but they can only ever learn something new when it relates to what they already know, when they already have some sort of internal mental representation to slot this new knowledge into. So what they already know will influence what knowledge they will acquire next, and babies do seem to progress through stages of knowledge in similar ways. Again it seems that genetics are driving development to unfold in a certain sequence which is then fine tuned by the environment.

The where and the what

It seems that your baby will spend quite a lot of the first year of her life coming to terms with objects. Initially she won't think about objects as you do, as things that continue to exist, but will think of objects either in terms of their motion or of their location, but not both. In fact this is not as strange as it might seem in that we register motion and detail in different parts of our eyes, this visual input then goes into different parts of our brain in two streams – one focusing on 'where' which develops first, and one focusing on 'what' which comes later. And babies are much better at sensing movement early on than on focusing on fine detail.

Object permanence

If a baby is presented with an object moving from centre to right and back again, by 12 weeks she can track this moving object, but if after a few moves, the object moves to the left and stops there, the baby continues to look to the right. Or if the object stops moving, she continues to look along the trajectory as if expecting to see it there even though it is perfectly visible. She's also completely unconcerned if the object suddenly disappears, or changes into something else; she doesn't search for the original object.

It is as if, for the first four to five months, she's seeing one object in terms of its motion and another in terms of its location, not seeing that both could actually be a single entity. She lacks the concept of 'object permanence'. If you cover up an object with a cloth, at this age your baby will look puzzled. Even if it is quite obvious to you that the object is underneath the cloth because you can see the cloth bulging, for some reason your baby cannot grasp this. If the cloth is transparent, she will happily pull it off and retrieve the desired object, so the problem is not one of co-ordination, but it is as if the baby thinks the object has gone when she cannot see it as it was before. This is because babies don't realize that things continue to exist when they can't see them: for your baby 'out of sight is out of mind' – literally!

Initially then, your baby will have limited vision. She will pay attention to the way things move and mostly ignore shape, colour or texture, though she will be very interested in contrast and the edges of objects. Later on she can take in these other details as her sight develops. As she gains experience she can begin to work out where objects begin and end – to differentiate things.

As she matures, she develops a deeper understanding of objects, which means she's developing internal representations of objects. As she starts to identify different, specific objects she can also begin to identify categories of objects. At around 18 months your baby will start sorting objects into piles according to say colour or shape, and this forming of categories allows language to really take off, though the understanding of language really starts when your child has object permanence, which allows her to understand that words can represent objects.

If you watch your baby carefully when she encounters something new, you can see her doing a fairly systematic but thorough exploration of an object:

- At around six to seven months, any new object is explored with all the senses, starting with the mouth. Once it has been explored your baby loses interest.
- By one year she will vary her actions; perhaps tapping and banging it.
- By eighteen months she will be pretty familiar with many objects, but if you now show her one with an unexpected property – perhaps it squeaks when held in a certain way, she will then systematically test it to see if it will do other things. At this stage she also starts to sort things of the same categories into piles.

The first internal representation – 'like me'

Having internal representations is very useful, because it allows you to organize your knowledge. Imagine being newborn and having no way of making sense of any of the input that you encounter; all those sights, sounds, smells, sensations. It would be overwhelming, but it is ok because babies' first internal representations are probably set up in the relatively calm environment of the womb, through hearing their mothers' voices and tasting their amniotic fluid. Thus at birth they listen out for human (particularly female) voices, and focus on familiar and sweet smells (amniotic fluid and breast milk) because these are things they have already experienced. Within a few days they will have learnt who is who and prefer to focus on familiar faces, voices and smells.

Babies know themselves from birth

From the moment of birth, babies know and prefer to look at human faces. If you stick your tongue out at your newborn baby, and if she is alert and interested, she will copy you.

Just think about this for a moment and what this implies. Your baby has not yet seen herself in a mirror, and even if she had, there is no way of explaining to her that the two dimensional representation she sees there is, in fact, herself. Yet she manages to copy you.

This means that somehow she is able to recognize that you are like her, that you are protruding something from your mouth and that she has a similar thing which she could also protrude. She is translating a visual image into an action. This amazing feat demonstrates that she is born, not only with an internal representation of her body, but also some sense that other people are 'like me'.

We also know that babies are aware of what a human face should look like and seek this out from the moment of birth, so this is innate. It takes them a good few years to figure out how people differ but they certainly have a sense of similarity. They look out for people and copy them from birth.

What babies know about other people

One experimenter, working with two-week-old babies, created a set up where babies could see either their mother or a stranger through a porthole over their cots. The babies preferred to look at their mother naturally enough. However, when the mother's lips moved but the stranger's voice came out (through an ingenious use of microphones), the babies were disturbed and tried to turn away from this upsetting incongruity. So it looks as if from an early age, babies have a sense of their mother as a person with a particular voice, face and so on.

Interestingly though, it seems that their concept of mother is not necessarily of a single person with continued existence. The same experimenter used mirrors so that babies would see multiple mothers, and found that young babies would happily interact with all three. It was not until babies were about five months old that they become upset when seeing multiple mothers.

This of course ties in with your baby's understanding of object permanence. In order to develop a sense of herself or indeed of someone else, your baby has to understand that she is a unique person distinct from other people, and that these other people continue to exist in the same way as she does.

This also fits in with what we looked at in Chapter 09 – the formation of attachments. It is not until about seven to nine months of age that babies develop separation anxiety, preferring one particular person; usually her mother. So perhaps until your baby knows that people continue to exist even when out of sight, she cannot have separation anxiety.

Imitation – the uniquely human behaviour

Babies imitate adults, even if the behaviour makes no sense to them. Consider how a baby will pick up a toy telephone and put the receiver to her ear, copying her parents even though she might not yet know what they get out of this act. And as an adult you will imitate your baby too – and in the process you will be moulding her future behaviour.

When your baby makes a face, you will find yourself copying her and elaborating on her action. Think about how you open your own mouth when spoon-feeding a baby, without even thinking about it. And babies love it when adults imitate them, often developing more and more elaborate behaviours just to see if the adult will follow suit. Babies will only imitate what makes some sort of sense to them though, they will not imitate actions that are too complex. It seems that they imitate what they are ready to use in this internal representational system.

- As your baby grows you can develop more elaborate turn-taking games which involve you imitating each other. In the early weeks, smiling and sticking your tongue out at each other will be very rewarding for each of you. Later on, you can do a peek-a-boo game where you close your eyes and open them slowly and watch your baby imitate you. When she is nearing the end of her first year, you can play peek-a-boo where you cover your eyes with your hands and she will now be able to copy you too.

Imitation is obviously an innate mechanism that humans – both adult and baby – use to aid learning. While this might seem obvious, it's not really, in that this form of learning is unique to our species. Most other animals do not appear to learn through this interaction of imitation.

Perhaps imitation is something that is linked to having a complex culture, as it allows us to absorb knowledge and skills which have been developed through cultural history. Or perhaps it is linked to consciousness or self-awareness; we can recognize ourselves in a mirror (as can chimps, bonobos and orangutans while most other primates and animals cannot). Self-recognition or self-awareness and imitation seem to be part of the same system – matching internal sensations to external events.

The pleasure of learning

Your baby will get tremendous pleasure from making things happen. One experimenter put mobiles over babies' cots; he set it up so that one group of babies had no control over the mobiles, while the second group could make the mobiles move by moving their cots. The babies who had control smiled and cooed while they were moving their mobiles, the other group of babies paid attention to the mobiles but did not coo or smile.

Psychologists refer to this as 'contingent' stimulation – meaning that for your baby, an event is stimulating and enjoyable when it follows some action of her own in an appropriate way, like a 'reply' to her action.

Most babies experience these contingent responses from their parents of course, and as we can see from the following experiment, these contingent responses really matter to them.

The experimenter set up a video link between babies and their mothers; in one situation the babies were interacting with their mothers in real time, in the other situation they were seeing a previously recorded video of their mothers. Even though the mothers in the recording were still talking to and smiling at them, the babies got very upset because this was now out of sync – the contingent responses were inappropriate.

Watch how your baby enjoys this 'contingent stimulation' either through interacting with you or through making things happen in other ways. For instance, you could try seeing how she reacts differently to having a balloon tied to her cot that you wiggle about, with having the same balloon tied to her ankle so she can control it.

When your baby is smiling and waving her arms around at you she is trying to 'talk' to you and your 'contingent response' would be to say something like, 'aren't you chatty today? Don't you have a lot to say?' and then pause and watch as she smiles and waves at you again. She will get really excited if you can carry on a 'conversation' like this.

Case study

Susan and Geoff are both professional musicians, and are keen to introduce their children to music as soon as possible. They are expecting their first baby, and Susan is already convinced that he or she can recognize certain pieces of music. Is there anything they can do to encourage musical ability in their children or will they inherit musicality anyway?

Susan is right – her baby will be recognizing certain pieces of music if they are played often enough, and already her baby is absorbing musicality simply by being exposed to music all the time. If Susan and Geoff continued to expose their baby to music, and then did a scan of her brain, they would find that more space is being devoted to music than in the brains of children who come from non-musical families.

Summary of this chapter

- Babies' brains are designed to grow in response to experience.
- Your baby will recognize all faces at first but in a general way, and over time hone in on recognizing particular faces that she sees more of. This helps her to develop some more subtle forms of communication, but also means she loses the ability to tell the difference between faces of people she does not have much exposure to.
- She increases her knowledge step by step, building on what she knows already and adding to it.
- Imitation is one particular way human beings learn from each other.
- Your baby will get great pleasure out of learning new things.

What this means for you and your baby

Babies thrive on interaction from the very beginning. You can have fun imitating your baby, and watching her imitate you in return. Try spending time in imitation games. Sit with your newborn baby very close to you (she can only focus on your face at a distance of about 8–12 inches). Stick your tongue out slowly and deliberately, and then wait. It may take up to a minute, but she should then copy you. You can try other things too like raising your eyebrows, or giving her a big smile – see how much she can do! She will get tired very easily though, so little and often is best.

Try experimenting with different objects to see what attracts your baby's attention at different ages. You will find that as a newborn she likes sharp contrast in big bold black and white patterns. Watch how she responds differently to moving or static objects. Try wearing a scarf or hat – you will probably get quite a blank expression!

See too what makes her smile at different ages and stages, and how big the smile is that she reserves for you!

She will also enjoy it if you are predictable. This is why people recommend you get into a routine. The best routine though, is one that suits both of you and involves a certain predictable pattern to your day, rather than trying to do everything by the clock. Bedtime routines, for instance, are a good way of winding down the day and will help your baby go off to sleep. Having routines around mealtimes are important for your developing family – most families find that eating together is an ideal way of sharing the day.

15

learning to communicate

In this chapter you will learn:
- why languages are so difficult to master
- how babies learn language from the moment they can hear
- that your child initially learns to communicate non-verbally
- the crucial role you play in teaching your child to speak.

Being able to communicate with words is perhaps the asset which makes us particularly unique in the animal kingdom, and arguably has led to our dominance as a species. Talking lets us share skills over generations and co-ordinate our actions allowing us to work effectively together. Within a few years of birth, children are part of a speaking culture, communicating effortlessly. How do they acquire language so quickly?

The problem of language

To understand just how amazing it is that your child will be a fluent speaker within a few years of birth, just think about visiting a foreign country and trying to understand what people are saying. How do you make sense of this stream of sound?

Scientists have struggled for years to find a way to programme computers to do what children do naturally – understand a conversation. The problem is we do not speak, as we write, with gaps between words; instead we produce a continuous stream of sound, with all the words flowing together. It's our brain which breaks this sound wave down into single sounds.

The other problem is that everyone's voice produces a slightly different sound; even a simple word like 'yes' will be different depending on: who says it; how quickly they say it; how loudly they speak; whether they are male or female; adult or child; their accent; the shape of their mouth and so on. Think of the difference between whispering, singing or shouting that single word 'yes' for instance. There are thousands of possible variations but our brain handles these and interprets everything without any conscious effort.

Even if we only had to ever listen to one voice, a small difference in the sound that voice makes can create a big difference in meaning. A pairing of a particular consonant with a particular vowel has one sound; the same consonant with a different vowel will produce a completely different sound wave.

So the poor computer can learn to understand spoken English only if the speaker uses very few words, each one separated by a pause, and even then it can cope with one voice only. By age three, in contrast, an English-speaking child can understand a language which contains over 75,000 words, spoken at normal speed by any number of different people.

How do they get there so quickly? The answer must be that babies are born already 'knowing' a great deal about how language works and with powerful learning mechanisms which allow them to add what they need in their particular society.

How babies learn to recognizze sounds

Sorting out that continuous stream of sounds begins in the womb, where foetuses are already actively listening and processing the sounds from outside. Hearing is fully developed at around 4¹/₂ months gestation and babies even in the womb respond positively to music they've heard before. They can recognize different stories as we saw earlier: experimenters got mothers to read *The Cat in the Hat* out loud twice a day during the last six weeks of pregnancy, and found that shortly after birth the babies preferred this story to another. Another researcher found that newborn babies stopped crying when they heard the theme from TV soaps their mothers had watched during pregnancy.

Babies of course don't understand *The Cat in the Hat* at birth or understand what the theme tune from *Eastenders* is about, but it seems that tuning into their own language means listening for repetitions. This is important as of course they don't know which language they are going to speak, so they need to focus in on what will be important for them.

Babies are born with the potential to learn any language, but this 'focusing in' helps them to pick out the sounds that are important, and eventually to ignore others, as one of the first tasks for your baby is to learn to recognize the sounds particular to his language, some of which might be unique – the Japanese do not have r and l, for instance.

Adults are quite culturally specific in listening to a language, but babies are not. To understand this, imagine recording the sound wave that is human speech on a piece of paper. It is virtually impossible to read the recording and say, 'there is an l or there is an r', yet we can hear these sounds distinctly. If you then use a speech synthesizer to gradually change the sound 'r' to 'l', although the synthesizer produces a range of sounds, which you could see changing on the graph paper, you will actually only hear 'r, r, r...' suddenly changing to 'l, l, l...' Japanese people won't hear the change at all – they continue to hear the same sound.

What happens is that each culture divides sounds into categories particular to them. So an English 'o' sounds different from a French 'o' or a Danish 'o'; indeed regional accents work like this too – think of the difference between a Scottish, Yorkshire and cockney 'a'.

Once we are used to our own language we won't hear the shifts from one vowel to another in other languages like Thai, or indeed the regional shifts within the same language that other nations hear, for instance Americans won't hear the shift between Yorkshire and cockney that we hear, whereas to us all American accents sound fairly similar. But babies can hear them all – Japanese babies hear the shift from 'r' to 'l', and English-speaking babies will hear the shifts in Thai, even if they have never heard these sounds before.

However, somewhere between six and 12 months the ability to discriminate all sounds has gone, and babies only notice sounds particular to their language. What is happening is that repeated exposure to particular sounds reinforces certain categories of sound and if you like, deletes others, and thus babies develop 'prototypes' of sounds. By paying attention to the words of their culture, they create an internal representation of the most typical 'r', most typical 'l' and so on, and somewhere between six and 12 months they have a store in their memory of culturally typical sounds. Sounds that they hear after that are compared to these prototypes and interpreted accordingly. This is why, despite the fact that hundreds of slightly different versions of 'd' might enter our ear, we will hear them all as one, prototypical 'd'.

Learning where words begin and end

So during the first year of life your baby is building up internal representations of typical sounds, which he needs to do before he can begin to learn what words mean. But he also needs to be able to notice where words begin and end. How does he do that when people talk in a stream of sound?

As well as tuning into the prototypical sounds of their own language, babies are paying attention to the rhythms of speech, so that by nine months, English-speaking babies have learnt that we emphasize the first syllable of every word (most other languages don't). They have also learnt which sound combinations are possible in their own languages. It is probable that babies are born ready to listen out for small segments of speech, like these stressed syllables, to pay attention to the melody and rhythm of speech and to notice the gaps before and after utterances.

> **Fascinating fact**
> *Babies go on listening in order to learn even when they are asleep!*
> A study in Finland split 45 newborn babies into three groups. The first group heard a tape of their mother chanting unusual vowel sounds as they slept, the second group heard common vowel sounds, and the third (control) group heard no tape. The following morning, the first group recognized the unusual vowel sounds, whereas the other two groups did not recognize them.

Earliest communication

Perhaps one of the reasons babies are so motivated to learn their native tongue is that language allows us to communicate, and babies are, above all, sociable.

While babies during their first year of life are busily acquiring the knowledge of sound and speech rhythms they will need to speak, they are also communicating non-verbally from the moment of birth and in the process, learning the skills they need to conduct a conversation; how to take turns, how to understand intention and so on.

We have seen that from birth your baby is interested in people and is above all attracted to the human face. We know that if you stick your tongue out at a newborn baby, he will imitate. What is your baby doing when he imitates you? It seems that he understands that you are making a social signal to which he wants to respond, even if at this stage it has no meaning for him at all.

The development of the smile

Apart from the intense and sustained eye contact and attempts to imitate you, the first really social response from your baby is probably the smile. Smiles appear very early on. The earliest smiles are referred to as 'endogenous', meaning they are triggered internally. You may spot your baby smiling in his sleep. These smiles appear around the mouth and cheeks, but don't really reach his eyes.

The earliest 'exogenous' smiles (smiles responding to external stimuli) appear around two weeks of age in response to people; experiments have shown that babies smile when they hear human voices but don't smile for other noises like a bell ringing. These smiles are still brief twitches of the mouth; the first real (though brief) smile occurs around three weeks of age, mostly in response to a female voice. By six weeks he smiles at a face, a prolonged smile involving his whole face which is generally called a social smile, and from then on he will smile at lots of different things.

Incidentally the reason your baby smiles in his sleep is because the motor neurons controlling the facial muscles involved in smiling are very close to the brainstem area that controls REM sleep.

Smiling happens in all cultures, and is inborn. Blind babies will smile even though they have nothing to copy; premature babies will smile later, at their conceptual age. The initial smile is instinctive but develops into an essential part of his social repertoire, so by three months the big 'smile of recognition' is reserved for his mother and father.

Interestingly though, although a blind baby starts smiling at the same age as a sighted baby, when they don't get the response from their parents – that visual interaction, their facial expressions become less responsive and less varied, while slighted children go on to produce more subtly different smiles to match occasions.

What is interesting is to observe how useful the smile is to your baby. It can express pleasure – 'how pleased I am to see you!' It expresses his sense of humour – babies seem to find incongruity funny – just as adults do. So 'Mummy making that face' is funny; surprising but non-threatening things are funny, making your baby smile and eventually also laugh.

Your baby's greatest joy though, is when he can make things happen, getting intellectual pleasure from discovering something. He also loves being able to anticipate events, which is why perhaps repetition of games like 'round and round the garden', are so wonderful for him. You can see an enormous smile as he waits, holding his breath, for the next go.

Interaction and turn-taking

Learning to communicate is not only about learning what words mean, but also how to hold a conversation. Humans don't just talk at each other, they take turns, they pay attention to what the person's body language is telling them too. Whole books have been written about body language, and although there is no firm agreement about exactly how much meaning we pick up non-verbally, psychologists would probably concur that it is at least 65 per cent. Communicating through body language and interpreting it is unconscious – often we can't say exactly why we don't trust what someone was telling us for instance, and it is probably mostly innate.

When two people from the same culture are talking to each other, their bodies are also moving in 'interactional synchrony' – mirroring each other's head and hand movements and general posture. You can tell how intimate people are by watching them talk together even if you cannot hear what they are saying, simply by observing this body language dance. You will probably only be aware of having learnt these specific movements when you encounter someone from a completely different culture and find talking to them 'awkward' when they hold eye contact too long or stand too close.

What is particularly interesting is that babies have been observed moving in synchrony with the human speech going on around them – whichever language it is – while they do not do this dance for non-speech sounds. They are also better at this dance when doing it with their own language rather than with a foreign language.

Your baby will learn the interactional synchronic movements specific to his culture, starting by developing a unique set of interactions with you, then with others in his close family, eventually being able to do it with all people in his own culture.

Babies actually seek out this interaction, making eye contact and small sounds, to which parents respond with eye contact and talking. It is often the baby who initiates this and the parent who responds. Most parents can't help but respond to this interaction, though depressed mothers are unable to respond as effectively and this is one very good reason why getting help for post-natal depression as soon as possible, is vital.

Sadly children who are in full-time care in day nurseries from an early age do not have as much experience of this interactional synchrony. Using video cameras and one-way mirrors, psychologists have rated the quality of interaction between carers and children at day nursery. Even when the carers know they are being observed, they do not do as good a job as parents.

There are fewer interactions, and these interactions are more mechanical, brusque and shorted in duration. They are just not as responsive, and this has an effect on the baby's social development.

So your baby will learn to communicate by firstly mastering a social world of non-verbal interaction onto which he 'maps' language.

- While breastfeeding, babies often pause in suckling to listen to their mother's voice, replying by sucking. These rhythms of suckling seem to be a precursor to conversation.
- Early on there is the exchange of eye contact (mutual gaze) and smiles.
- This leads to the development of joint attention. At six months, babies will follow their mother's gaze to see what she is looking at.
- Shared gestures: by nine months babies will start pointing at objects to communicate. They will reach for an object while looking at their mother, thus saying non-verbally, 'give that to me!' This 'joint attention' stage is crucial – mothers will now name objects that they are both paying attention to, and thus the baby can start to copy and accumulate a vocabulary of named objects.
- Games like 'Peek-a-boo' with a ritual pattern suggest the give and take of a conversation.

'Motherese' – the language of parenting

When we come face to face with a baby, we all do it, we put on a silly voice. Sometimes you become a little self-conscious, becoming aware how daft you must sound to other adults. However, psychologists now think that this silly voice is a powerful, innate mechanism which all human beings use in order to help children to speak.

Motherese is perhaps a misnomer, because all adults use it when faced with babies: mothers, fathers, even people without children. It is found in other cultures, and it works in a very specific way. Firstly the voice rises, as much as an octave or even higher, the pitch varies while talking so it is melodic – 'sing-songy' – sentences are shorter and simpler, there is a lot of repetition, consonants are formed properly rather than slurred or skipped and vowels are exaggerated, so overall the speech is slower and more distinct.

Motherese uses concrete nouns and proper nouns, avoiding pronouns and conjunctions, and will usually refer to what is happening here and now.

Remembering how hard it is to distinguish words in a stream of sound, Motherese seems to be a particularly effective tool in helping babies to focus on the words of their culture. As we saw, babies take notice of the silences in order to identify words; Motherese is spoken in a way that is particularly helpful for babies at this stage. Researchers have also noticed that mothers instinctively put more emphasis on new words when talking to their children at the age when they are primed to acquire vocabulary. And when babies are younger their mothers emphasize the vowels of their own language in exactly the right way to allow their babies to develop the right prototypes for their language.

How you will teach your baby to speak

Building on turn-taking, exchanging smiles and playing games, parents are also working with their babies' vocalizations, interpreting them and imposing meaning on them.

Your baby will probably first start to vocalize at around three months with general cooing – vowel sounds like oooh, ahhh, and researchers have suggested that what he is doing is creating a sort of internal map of 'sound to mouth shape', copying the vowels he has heard and practising them. He will probably combine these vowel sounds with facial expressions and hand and finger movements, looking for all the world as though he is desperate to say something. Psychologists call this protoconversation or prespeech. Your response – cooing back and talking, introduces your baby to the world of turn-taking vocal dialogue.

- At three months, when your baby does this cooing and waving his arms around, respond as if he is trying to talk to you, and talk back; copy his facial expressions, interpret his sounds and gestures into words. Although it might feel 'silly' you will be encouraging him to continue to communicate and thus helping him learn to talk.

Around seven to eight months (when if you remember, babies have developed the prototypical vowel) he will start to string consonant and vowel together into a stream of babble, practising that intricate co-ordination needed to speak. Although as an adult it feels effortless to talk (and more so for some than others, you might think) it does require quite intricate co-ordination of several muscles controlling lips, tongue, palate and larynx. So your baby will be practising saying things like babababababa or mamamama or dadadada at this stage. Whether your baby means anything or not by these sounds is a matter of debate among psychologists but you will certainly be tempted to attribute meaning to these sounds – 'listen, he is saying Mummy!' – and in most cultures the childhood name for the person who is usually the primary caregiver sounds very like that first babble (Mummy, Maman, Mutti etc).

- At this age when he starts to string together syllables, talk back to him, elaborate on what he is saying, interpret the sounds into something meaningful. Again this is not being silly but is part of helping him to acquire language. For instance when he goes, 'mummuummuumm' you can respond by saying something like, 'Mummy! Yes here is Mummy! Mummy is here and we are going to play now! What is Mummy doing? Mummy is going to tickle your tummy!'

Parents continue to assume baby's shared knowledge of words (and it is certainly true that children understand far more than they can say) and continue to shape their baby's vocabulary by attributing meaning to their utterances.

- When he is about a year old, you'll fine yourself giving a running commentary on his actions, which might feel insane, but it is an extremely important, natural way of teaching his to speak. 'Are you giving me that cup? Yes, you are giving me that cup. What a helpful boy' and so on.

A cause perhaps for embarrassment if done in front of other adults, but something parents do spontaneously and naturally when faced with a child of that age. And yet what adults are doing here is teaching their children culturally specific meanings.

They are also focusing on what is important to understand about that language; so Korean-speaking mothers, in order to help their children get to grips with all the different verb endings conveying different meanings, will emphasize verbs often omitting nouns, while English-speaking mothers will focus on nouns more.

Meanwhile the babies are now combining different syllables and consonants into long complex babbles – by 12 months they can produce most of the vowels and about half of the consonant sounds in English (it takes several years to grasp the more complex sounds like 'th', 'bl' and 'gr')

Acquiring language – ages and stages

- First 6–12 months – learning prototypical sounds, practising prototypical vowels in babbling around three months, practising prototypical vowel and consonant combination (dadada) around eight months.
- Around 12 months – first words produced (it is easy to miss these). From now on babbling will sound culturally specific: English-speaking babies will sound English when they babble.
- Up to 18 months toddlers use single words with great flexibility, applying the same word to many objects with an internal logic. 'Dada' for all men for instance, 'dog' might be used to describe all animals or perhaps all moving objects or brown things – whatever makes sense and is useful to the baby.
- At 18 months and beyond there is a rapid accumulation of vocabulary, with your child pointing at everything and asking for its name, referred to as 'fast mapping'. Children typically have only about 20 words at 18 months but this has increased to an average of 200 by about 21 months. Seems too that words acquired at this age are remembered for a long time. Between the ages of two and six, children are estimated to learn eight new words a day, so that at age six they understand some 13,000 words (thought they won't use them all).
- As vocabulary increases, children start combining words into phrases, usually two-word 'telegraphic' speech – so called as it sounds like a telegram, for example, 'dog gone', 'shoe off'. Note that this telegraphic speech is usually in the grammatically correct order, so they don't say 'gone dog.' Single words can also be used to express ideas, referred to as 'holophrases' – typically 'more' actually means 'can I have some more of that please', for instance.
- By two years, children are regularly stringing three or four words together, using grammatical rules.
- Somewhere between three and five years your child will probably have a vocabulary of over 1,000 words, and will be able to carry on conversations, though the topic of conversation will still be rooted in the here and now.

Case study

Amelie and Pierre are both French but now live permanently in the UK. They can both speak fluent English, but are wondering which language to use with their new baby, and whether their baby will be confused if they speak to him or her in both French and English.

Babies are capable of learning two or even more languages simultaneously – in fact it is a great gift that Amelie and Pierre can give to their child; the gift of being truly bilingual.

They may find that their baby is a little slower to speak than children who are only absorbing one language, but she or he will quickly catch up, and will show very little confusion. A bilingual baby might occasionally address someone in the wrong language, but they never muddle up the vocabulary so that a sentence is a mixture of the two, which shows a remarkable grasp of the separateness of the two languages.

Interestingly, most women find it easier to talk to their babies in their own native tongue, and find it very hard or unnatural to speak to their babies in Motherese in a second language.

Summary of this chapter

- Learning to speak is not as easy as it might seem, yet babies grasp it seemingly effortlessly.
- Babies are born ready to understand any language they may encounter.
- They have very good hearing so that they can begin to absorb their native tongue long before they are born.
- Babies are born with inbuilt learning mechanisms, to pay attention to speech; to listen out for rhythms, patterns and repetitions.
- However, adults too have inbuilt mechanisms driving us to teach children in ways that will work exactly as needed.

What this means for you and your baby

During pregnancy, you can set up calming associations for your baby. Play soothing music to your baby, sing to him, and when he is born, you may find that the music and songs will comfort him when he is fractious.

Once your baby is born, having conversation going on around him will help him tune into language and get ready to speak.

When your baby is little, notice how he wants to take turns with you, and that he has a sense of timing and rhythm that tunes in with yours. You could almost say your baby flirts with you!

Play games with your baby, like 'Round and round the garden', or 'Peek-a-boo' whenever your baby seems alert. Nappy-changing time is usually good, or as you get your baby undressed for the bath.

Talk to your baby, both before and after birth, as much as you can. He will be paying attention to your every word, and you will be giving him a head start in language acquisition. At first, this can feel a bit silly – try starting with a running commentary on what you are doing 'look, I'm loading the washing machine... haven't you got lots of dirty clothes... the machine is going to make lots of whooshing noise in a minute...' Once you have done it for a while, you will feel less self-conscious, especially when you see how much your baby loves it.

Notice how you use Motherese without thinking, or notice how your partner does! Try not to feel self-conscious about this – just remember how much you are helping your child to speak.

play

In this chapter you will learn:
- why babies play
- what we mean by play
- that play is a vital part of childhood, a tool for learning about the physical and social world.

From the very beginning your baby will play. When she shakes a rattle or drops her toys from her pram, she is not only having fun, she's also absorbing some elementary physics. We know that adults usually absorb new things more easily if they actively participate in their learning; we would find it almost impossible to learn to drive a car by only reading a manual, for instance, but for young children, activity *is* learning.

The purpose of play in the natural world

The ability to adapt to our surroundings is what makes human beings so successful, and playful behaviour is a big part of this adaptive learning. It is interesting that animals with bigger brains relative to their body size spend significantly more time playing than animals with smaller brains. In fact, most of the more intelligent species play; kittens and puppies play rough and tumble, and pretend to capture balls of string, but ants and bees just get on with life.

The more flexible and adaptable a species, the more they play. This is the 'flexibility complex' which includes a long period of maturation and dependency on adult caregivers, an ability to manipulate objects, learning by observation, and the development of peer groups in the young of the species and social structures within adolescence.

Play is 'experimental dialogue' in that you can take back what is said or done. So it lets the young of a species try out new behaviour in a familiar situation, or familiar behaviour in a new situation. Play declines with age in all species (although adults will play with offspring) suggesting that it is about learning and early development, and apes and humans play for longer and take longer to develop than all the other mammals. Play is quite similar to exploration – indeed play with other young is partly exploratory. Humans have the most complex play of all animals: while kittens can be seen to be practising the skills they will need as adult cats, children's play is more complex and seems to have other functions too.

In evolutionary terms, play could even be seen as fairly dangerous – young animals who are very involved in playing may be unaware of an approaching predator for instance, so play must be adaptive behaviour. For instance, 80 per cent of deaths among young fur seals occur because the playful pups fail to spot approaching predators. So the dangers of playful exploration must be offset by the benefits the animal gains through learning.

For human beings, early childhood is the time when our imaginations are the most fertile, we can make links between objects far more freely – for instance imagining that a broom is a weapon or a blade of grass is spinach, because our brains can create more associations; the more experience we have the more our thinking runs in particular pathways. Once we have strong internal representations we censor odd thoughts far more so that we cannot undertake imaginative play so freely – we replace imagination with knowledge, we replace magic and superstition with understanding.

What is play?

Play can be defined as something that is enjoyable, that does not necessarily have a definite goal or end result (although games for older, school-age children which have rules, like football or Monopoly, would have more definite goals). It is spontaneous and voluntary – children choose to play, and usually decide for themselves what to play – and it is active (unlike, for instance, watching TV or reading a book).

What does play do for children?

Play seems to have several functions. Partly it is about modelling adult behaviour and thus learning about the world. You could also say it is partly about letting off steam and having fun, but play can also be 'cathartic': children often express worries and work through problems or anxieties in their play, and indeed child therapists often use play in their diagnostic and therapeutic work. However, play is initially social – children need adults to play with initially, then other children, and solitary or fantasy play develops out of these early social interactions. Children who play well have better social skills than other children though not necessarily improved cognitive skills, so play has a social rather than cognitive purpose.

How play develops

For the first two years of life, your baby's play is mostly in the here and now; manipulating objects and experiencing or experimenting with objects through the various senses. For your baby at this stage, the pleasure comes from being able to control things, making things happen. She is experimenting all the time; what does this feel like in my mouth? What happens when I do this? There is a great sense of satisfaction in making things reoccur.

You will probably find that you play with your baby all the time without even thinking about it. Changing her nappy, you may blow raspberries on her tummy. 'Pat-a-cake', 'Round and round the garden'; all of these familiar action rhymes might become part of your repertoire. As we have seen your baby is not a passive recipient of these activities, but will be controlling and directing you too, by eye contact and gaze.

Do babies need toys?

You don't need to provide an enormous selection of toys for your baby, and sometimes really expensive toys are less valuable for your child's development than the simpler and cheaper toys. A very elaborate toy may have little flexibility in play; whereas a toy which allows your child plenty of scope is better.

Most people think play is just about interacting with toys – and indeed the earliest play is often with objects. Initially a baby plays with objects simply to learn about them. While toys are designed to be appealing, babies are interested in any objects, especially new ones, and will give each object a thorough examination with all the senses at her disposal. Your baby will often imitate what she has seen you do with an object, either immediately or even days afterwards. Delayed imitation is only possible when the baby can store a mental representation of an object; early repetition of action depends on a sensory memory – remembering what it felt like to do something.

Once your child moves into toddlerhood, objects still remain fascinating, but now they can also be used for being sociable. Firstly, they are something to communicate with Mum about through shared looking, pointing and so on. Then they become useful for parallel play with other children.

Early on babies are not skilled enough to interact with other children, but they will enjoy parallel play – being alongside another child playing in the sandpit for instance, or sitting in a box together and so on. Direct involvement with the same toy is the most common type of play in two-year-olds, and toys are important for social exchanges, giving, receiving and sharing (or snatching!). A toy that is owned by another child is doubly interesting of course, as are their reactions when the precious possession is seized.

So babies don't need particular toys, but they do need objects to play with. There are three broad functions for these:

- They are a means of expressing feelings or emotions. Toys can represent things, can allow your child to act out situations, but this will happen much later in life, when imaginative play really gets going at around 2–3 years of age.
- They are channel for communication. Having an object of interest allows children to interact with other children or adults, to discuss things, to take turns, and so on. This starts to happen about at the end of the first year.
- They are used to learn. Manipulating objects allows children to develop concepts, for instance, pouring sand and water out of containers allows children to understand about movement and gravity. Metal things make a particular noise when they bang together; wooden things make another type of noise. Exploratory play is what is most important for a baby, so concentrate on these types of toys at this stage.

Exploratory play

For exploratory play your child should have toys she can manipulate – bricks, posting boxes, as well as sand and water. It may look like mucking about, but at this age, your child learns about the world with her whole body. She learns about objects by examining them, discovering how things behave, about measurement weight and proportion. Cause and effect are unknown to the pre-schooler; rules we take for granted about the world are absorbed at this age, for instance, if you turn on a tap, water will always come out of it, if you drop a ball onto a hard surface, it will always bounce.

Creative play

Playing with paint, sand, glue and paper gives children lots of positive experiences. Experimenting with the physical properties of different materials gives them ideas about form and construction. As your baby gets older, the opportunity to create something unique, to have control over a project from beginning to end, is tremendously satisfying.

Creativity feeds into fantasy and make believe, initially though she just needs it to explore different materials – think of it as elementary physics!

Your reaction to your child's efforts will affect her creative play. Using slowed down videotapes, researchers noticed that young children were being directed in their painting by subtle positive and negative reactions from their mothers. So if you are likely to be freaked out by mess then make sure you have covered up table, chairs, floor, yourself and baby before you start!

Your role in your child's play

If play is natural and spontaneous, do children need to learn to play? Well we have seen that, for instance, creative play will be encouraged or suppressed in your child depending on your reactions; this has also been found to be true of all other types of play including imaginative play, which is tremendously important for language skills and expanding children's thinking. So make sure you play with your child – not only will it be fun, it will be helping her development.

Books for babies

To develop abstract and organized thought, your baby needs to acquire a large and complex vocabulary – and what better way, than reading? After all, your baby will pick up everyday words like hello, bye, juice and shoes, but how many chances does he have to experience what a giraffe is, what being lost means, or what a doctor does, apart from through books? Books offer you the chance to share exciting experiences without leaving the house.

During the early years, your baby is at her most receptive. Establishing that books are interesting and entertaining is best done now, so that she's more likely to want to learn to read when she's older.

How to read with your baby

It's never too soon to start reading to your baby. If you find Motherese artificial or strange, reading can help. If you are returning to work and feel that the time spent with your baby is going to be precious, use it productively by settling down for a cuddle and a read.

Books can become part of your bedtime routine, spending some calm, happy time together before sleeping, although don't reserve reading for bedtime; make time for a quiet session during the day as well. Begin by turning the pages slowly and naming the pictures. You are tuning your baby into the concept of two-dimensional representations of real life objects, and also that books read from front to back, left to right. As you progress into stories, don't worry about following the text strictly; use it as suits you and your baby. You will find as she get older, she constantly interrupts and asks questions, and this is fine. Books should be launching pads for ideas.

Getting your baby interested in books

Some households treat books as precious items to be handled delicately. This approach can wait. Right now you want your baby to explore books, which might mean torn or eaten pages. It also means books need to be accessible. By all means store expensive or precious books on a shelf out of reach, but everyday books should be in the toy box, where she can pick them up and handle them.

Using your local library

If you have not visited a library for some time, you will find they are no longer a place of enforced silence where children are, at best, tolerated. Most libraries now have a special section where noise is OK, and where books are stored in large, easily accessible boxes, with child-friendly chairs or floor cushions nearby. Use your library to the full, and when your baby is older she will love to choose her own books. Any books that become favourites can go on the Christmas list, because the best books will be read over and over again.

What to look for in a book

A good principle to follow for toy-box books is little books for little hands. Many parents start their babies off with board, rag or plastic books, as these stand chewing and drooling a bit better, and can be washed. These should be age-appropriate, with simple pictures and little or no text; keep stories for when your baby progresses onto real, paper books.

There are some great touchy, feely baby books available which invite rattling, chewing and generally getting involved. As they get older, lift the flap or noisy books are great for children who are on the go and easily bored, but make sure they are really sturdy; these books are useless when flaps are torn off.

In the beginning, illustrations are more important than text, and bright, simple pictures; Dick Bruna's for instance, are brilliant for babies. Drawings are often better than photographs as the illustrator can leave out complicated detail, and create a better two-dimensional representation. Babies need to create categories of objects – prototypes if you like: an example of the fire engine prototype is 'big and red with wheels and a ladder'. A photo, with all the extra paraphernalia of hoses, grills etc, could actually be less recognizable than a plain, simple brightly coloured drawing.

The effect of television

Some parents think TV is a good thing as it is exposing their children to language. While babies are born to communicate, unfortunately TV can't teach them to talk. For a start, the language used is often too complex. Speech therapists advise parents to limit TV viewing as children can even learn to ignore speech as they concentrate on the visual. Learning to speak involves active, two-way communication, not possible with the TV, but an essential part of reading with your baby.

Case study

Hannah has lots of brightly coloured toys to play with both at home and at the little mother and baby group her mum Siobhan attends. Her favourite 'toys' of all though, are her mum's keys. She loves to shake them and examine each key in turn in her mouth. Siobhan is worried about this because she is sure they are covered in germs and might be too sharp, and a couple of times there has been a panic when the keys were lost.

It's not surprising the keys are fascinating; they are shiny, make an interesting noise when you shake them, there are different textures and shapes to them, AND they also seem to have social significance.

By the time your baby is putting everything in her mouth there is less need to worry about sterilizing stuff, though of course toys should be reasonably clean and safe. Siobhan though, could create a special set of keys for Hannah from older keys which are well washed and have been examined for safety, and put them on an extra large, extra strong keyring, with perhaps some other interesting objects. That way there will be less panic if they disappear!

Summary of this chapter

- Play is common to the intelligent species and is an important part of development.
- Your encouragement will help your child to be playful and experimental.
- For babies, play is mostly about exploring objects on their own or with you, but they also love interactive games like 'Peek-a-boo' etc.
- Books are useful even for babies in helping them to talk, but TV should be limited at this age.

What this means for you and your baby

When you play a repetitive action game like 'Round and round the garden, notice how your baby responds, how she look at you to make you repeat your actions. Play with noise when you interact with her; making popping and tickling noises is not just mucking about, it is encouraging her to be creative too.

Don't spend all your money on large, elaborate toys. Instead invest in some simple bricks or shape sorters, and collect a variety of household objects for her to explore. Just bring a few things out at a time and change them round frequently. Watch her figure out cause and effect, how things work. A bucket of sand or water on the floor with a few spoons and cups will provide hours of entertainment.

gender differences

In this chapter you will learn:
- whether the differences between boys and girls are innate
- what differences are present at birth
- how fathers and mothers react differently to their children according to their sex.

We saw in Chapter 14 how babies develop a sense of self. It's incredible but true that even before your baby learns to talk, let alone play with toys, he knows what sex he is.

When you became a parent, the first question everyone asked was whether you had a boy or girl so they could inundate you with cards and flowers of the 'correct' colour – pink or blue.

Whether you desperately longed for a particular sex, or whether you felt it really didn't matter, there's no escaping the fact that as far as the rest of the world is concerned, your baby's sex is the most important aspect of his character and personality.

While it may not be the most important thing for your baby, and indeed it is not until well into pre-school years that children actually acquire a fixed gender identity, he will be able to spot the difference early on. Babies as young as ten months spend more time looking at pictures of babies the same sex as themselves. They can also spot a baby of the same sex by the way he moves, regardless of hairstyles or clothing.

How your baby sees men and women

By the time your baby is two months old, he will tend to react differently to his parents, his body language getting jerky and excited, holding himself stiffly, expecting to play when he sees his father. One paediatrician who writes about child development claims that if we block our vision so we can only see a toe, finger, hand or foot, we adults can still tell whether the baby is interacting with his mother or father.

Six-month-old babies are more worried by hearing a strange male voice than a strange female voice. They also prefer to look at the photograph of a woman's face to a man's face. By eight to nine months of age, when he is developing fear of strangers, he will prefer a strange female to a strange male.

- Lots of interacting with his father will help though; if babies spend lots of with their father, they will be far less scared of all strangers.

Differences between baby boys and baby girls

Sometimes it seems we are almost too keen to spot boyish or girlish traits in tiny babies, when really there is little to tell them apart except for the obvious genital difference.

Boys and girls do have slightly different growth patterns; the average boy at birth is slightly longer and heavier than the average girl, while the average girl is usually born with a bit more fat. In the beginning your baby will grow faster if he's a boy, but at seven months, girls speed up, growing faster than boys until about four years of age. Girl babies' vision develops faster than boys. Things are pretty even from then until puberty, when once again girls race ahead for a few years. These differences are only statistical however, and individual boys and girls vary enormously.

One experimenter worked with 13-month-old children, and noticed that at play they showed some sex differences in that the girls were more reluctant to move far from their mothers, returning to them for more reassurance than the boys. When a gate was erected which prevented the babies from reaching their mothers, the girls stood and cried helplessly, while the boys, although they cried too, made vigorous attempts to break down the barrier.

It was also noticeable that while both sexes at this age chose toys to manipulate rather than to 'pretend' and were happy to chose the same kind of toys, they used them in different ways: the boys preferred more active play with lots of banging and running about, while the girls tended to sit and play, and only the girls picked cuddly animals while only the boys chose hammers and lawnmowers.

Similarities outweigh differences in infancy though, and only become stronger and more marked in types of play, choice of toys etc. as children grow older. By the time your baby starts nursery, the contrasts will be far more obvious. Eventually, statistically speaking, boys will tend to be more aggressive and tend to develop better spatial skills, while girls will tend to be better with language. Socially, boys will play in gangs while girls have one or two close friends.

Are sex differences inborn?

The 'nature versus nurture' argument really becomes heated when you apply it to sex differences. Given that babies start off fairly similar and that sex differences become more exaggerated as they grow older, are they simply responding to peer pressure, or are they born to behave the way they do?

Are boys born to be aggressive?

Is your tiny baby boy inevitably going to grow up to be a noisy and aggressive thug? Unfortunately this is more likely to happen than if you have a girl. In almost every culture that has been studied, from toddlerhood boys are more aggressive than girls, not only physically, but also verbally – they use more taunts and insults. It used to be thought that boys learn to be aggressive through being given toy guns and soldiers to play with while girls had their natural aggression suppressed. However, if this were true, we would expect girls to express this suppressed aggression in safe, fantasy games, but this doesn't happen. Parents discourage aggression in both sexes, even coming down harder on this sort of behaviour in boys, so we are not subtly teaching boys that aggression is OK.

- Encourage your daughter to get involved in physical sports as soon as she can; take her swimming or to baby gym, and make a point of getting involved in rough and tumble with her too.

Are girls born to be chatterboxes?

Cartoons suggest females talk all the time at silent, sulky partners. It's true that in general your newborn baby girl enjoys hearing your voice almost more than being cuddled, whereas your newborn baby boy would definitely choose a cuddle every time.

At only one to three days of age, baby girls respond more to social cues like a human voice or face than baby boys; they smile twice as much as baby boys, and maintain eye contact (which is an important part of holding a conversation) with a silent adult twice as long as boys. Perhaps this explains why you might find yourself tending to talk to your baby more often if she is female, and picking him up and playing more boisterously with him if he is a boy.

Baby girls start babbling earlier than baby boys, but we don't know whether this would happen naturally, or whether it is because we encourage our baby girls to speak more; for instance within 48 hours of birth, mothers talk and smile more often to their baby girls, and pick up, cuddle and play more boisterously with their baby boys.

- Make sure you talk with your baby boy as much as possible, to develop his language skills.

Will you treat your baby differently?

- Fathers are often more affected by the sex of their baby than mothers, touching their newborn sons more than their daughters and being especially attentive to first-born boys. Fathers also tend to talk twice as much to their daughters than to their sons.

- Some fathers have more rigid ideas about what is acceptable behaviour for their sons and daughters, being horrified, for instance, if their son wants to push a dolly's pushchair around, while mothers seem more relaxed about this.

- Both parents do, however, teach 'boys to be boys' by stimulating them to be active and outgoing, even discouraging many of their attempts at communication, while at the same time encouraging their daughters to chatter.

Studies have shown that boys will become more like their fathers if they are warm and friendly, rather than cold and distant. Sons of bossy fathers tend to be disliked at playgroups and have behaviour problems later on. Sons of over-protective mothers, on the other hand, will grow up to be very compliant. Girls tend to grow up compliant if they suffer from excessive or harsh discipline.

You may think that you will treat your daughter or son simply in the way he or she wants to be treated, but in fact you will probably be responding to your own sex-role ideas. One experimental situation dressed babies randomly in sex-appropriate clothes, so that some boys were dressed as boys, but others were dressed as girls, and some girls were dressed as girls, but the others as boys. The researchers then asked mothers to play with a baby they had never seen before, and were told (often untruthfully) that the baby was a girl or boy. The mothers chose a hammer for the 'boy' babies to play with, and a doll for the 'girls'. What was even more interesting was that the mothers interpreted exactly the same behaviours differently according to which sex they believed the baby was. If the baby got restless and wriggly, they believed the 'boys' wanted to play, whereas they believed the 'girls' were upset and needed soothing.

Babies are of course influenced by many people, not just their parents. If this were not the case, then children brought up by one parent would suffer from gender identity problems. Men and women are just as good at handling babies and men raise their voices higher like women to speak to babies. Single parent fathers, as well as fathers who have the main childcare responsibilities while mum works, will tend to become more 'motherly'. In fact, our ability to look after children is one area in which there are really few sex differences. Your toddler, whether boy or girl, will enjoy feeding, bathing, and nursing baby dolls. As boys grow older, playing with dolls becomes taboo, yet one researcher got children to listen to a tape of a crying baby and found that, although girls seemed more concerned, the boys' 'concealed responses' – their blood pressure, heart beat etc. – were the same as the girls, so both sexes find a crying baby stressful and want to help.

Case study

Joanna is keen for her daughter Megan to grow up to be an independent girl with lots of options. Since becoming pregnant she has noticed how much the toy shops seem to stereotype toys into pink dolls for girls and war toys for boys, and feels appalled by all this. Should she keep Megan away from all this?

Joanna does seem right that we have really become very stereotyped in our choices of toys for children; however, early on babies won't express the preferences they will make later when they are more subject to peer pressure. In the meantime try to choose toys which are age appropriate and will stimulate their play (see previous chapter) rather than worrying about whether they are gender appropriate.

Summary of this chapter

- Differences between boys and girls are present at birth, but become more marked as children grow older.
- Parents also subtly influence their children to behave in ways expected of each gender – fathers possibly more so than mothers.

What this means for you and your baby

- Baby girls' visual-spatial skills can be encouraged with shape sorters, stacking and nesting toys and lift out puzzle trays. Progress from here to Duplo and later Lego or Meccano.
- Help your baby boy develop pre-language skills, including turn-taking and imaginative play. Make an effort to talk to him and interact in games like 'Peek a boo'. You can develop his imaginative play, for example, with a tea party for a favourite teddy.
- Books are crucial in developing a wide vocabulary, but you need to get children hooked on reading early – see previous chapter.
- You don't need to buy boys' toys for girls or vice versa. It is much better to use the toys your child already likes and to develop different skills and ways of playing.

taking it further

Resources

Benefits and legal advice

Citizens advice bureau, for help with benefits and legal issues:
www.citizensadvice.org.uk

Breastfeeding

NCT breastfeeding line 0870 444 8708, open 8 am to 10 pm.
Also for hire of breast pumps.

Childminding

www.ncma.org.uk – Childminding in England and Wales.

http://www.childminding.org – Scottish childminding
association.

Crying babies

Cry-sis offers support for families with excessively crying,
sleepless and demanding babies. Phone 08451 228 669, seven
days a week 9 am to 10 pm for an answering service which
gives you the phone number of volunteer contacts, who once
had similar problems: www.cry-sis.org.uk.

If you've reached the end of your tether or simply want
someone to talk to, call the NSPCC Child Protection Helpline
on 0808 800 5000. They have trained counsellors available 24
hours a day, seven days a week to offer parents and carers the
advice and support they need: www.nspcc.org.uk.

Parents' relationships

National Childbirth Trust offers antenatal, breastfeeding and post-natal classes, local post-natal support groups, nearly-new sales and many other services. Call 0870 444 8707 for the NCT helpline or visit **www.nctpregnancyandbabycare.com**.

The Parent Connection aims to encourage you to think about the importance of your relationship with your child's other parent, whether or not you are still together, and the impact this has on your child: **www.theparentconnection.org.uk**.

Several related websites are also helpful:

One plus one website has information and tips to help you to deal with things that may affect your relationship and also other sources of information and support: **www.oneplusone.org.uk**.

For more information on relationships, the legal differences between marriage and cohabitation and how to manage conflict in parental relationships, visit our family of websites:

www.theparentconnection.og.uk
www.marriedornot.org.uk
www.mymumanddadarguealot.org.uk

Parentline Plus is a national charity that works with parents to offer help and support through an innovative range of free, flexible, responsive services – shaped by parents for parents. Parentline Plus: 0808 800 2222, **www.parentlineplus.org.uk**.

Stepfamily Helpline Scotland: 0845 1228655

Post-natal depression

The Association for Post-Natal Illness provides a information leaflets for sufferers and healthcare professionals as well as a network of volunteers (telephone and postal), who have themselves experienced post-natal illness. Helpline (UK) 020 7386 0868, or **www.apni.org**.

Premature babies

Tommys for premature babies: 0870 777 30 60, **www.tommys.org**.

BLISS, call 0500 618140, Monday to Friday, 10 am to 5 pm. Outside these hours, you can leave a message on an ansaphone and they will return your call with 24 hours: **www.bliss.org.uk**.

Single parent families

Gingerbread is a support organization for over 1.8 million lone parents and their children throughout England and Wales: **www.gingerbread.org.uk**

National council for one-parent families is merging with Gingerbread. Currently they can help with childcare, employment, money issues, children's behaviour, useful organizations and more. Call 0800 018 5026, Monday to Friday, 9 am to 5 pm, Wednesdays 9 am to 8 pm, or visit **www.oneparentfamilies.org.uk**.

Twins and multiple births

TAMBA (Twins And Multiple Births Association) publish leaflets and booklets on all aspects of looking after twins or more. They can put you in touch with your local **twins club,** and run **Twinline,** a national, confidential support, listening and information service for all parents of twins, triplets and more. 10 am to 1 pm and 7 pm to 10 pm every day: 0800 138 0509, **www.tamba.org.uk**.

Recommended reading

Steve Biddulph (2006) **Raising Babies** – Should under 3s go to nursery? Thorsons.

Caroline Deacon (2002) The NCT book of **Breastfeeding for Beginners.** Thorsons.

Caroline Deacon (2004) **Babycalming** – simple solutions for a happy baby. Thorsons.

Lisa Eliot (1999) **Early Intelligence** – how the brain and mind develop in the first five years of life. Penguin.

Sue Gerhardt (2004) **Why love matters** – how affection shapes a baby's brain. Routledge.

Sally Goddard Blythe (2005) **The well balanced child** – movement and early learning. Hawthorn Press.

Alison Gopnik, Andrew Metlzoff and Patricia Kuhl (1999) **How babies think** – the science of childhood. Weidenfeld & Nicolson.

Lynne Murray and Liz Andrews (2005) **The Social Baby** – understanding babies' communication from birth. The Children's Project.

Naomi Stadlen (2004) **What mothers do** – especially when it looks like nothing. Piatkus.

To find out more about evolution and human development, or the 'nature versus nurture' argument see:

William H. Calvin (1998) **How brains think** – the evolution of intelligence. Phoenix.

Susan A. Greenfield (2000) **The private life of the brain.** Allen Lane.

Hilary and Steven Rose (eds.) **Alas Poor Darwin** – Arguments against Evolutionary Biology. Jonathan Cape.

Robert Winston (2002) **Human Instinct.** Bantam Press.

To read more about attachment theory see:

John Bowlby (1965) **Child Care and the Growth of Love** (2nd ed.) Penguin.

Sir Richard Bowlby (2004) **Fifty years of attachment theory** – the Donald winnicott memorial lecture. Karnac books.

Michael Rutter (1972) **Maternal Deprivation Reassessed.** Penguin.

For more about your baby's sensory world and how to comfort your baby:

Caroline Deacon (2004) **Babycalming** – simple solutions for a happy baby. Thorsons.

Megan Faure and Ann Richardson (2002) **Baby Sense.** Metz Press.

Lynne Murray and Liz Andrews (2005) **The Social Baby** – understanding babies' communication from birth. The Children's Project.

For more about twins see:

Elizabeth Bryan (1995) **Twins, Triplets and More** – their nature, development and care. Multiple Births Foundation.

Alessandra Piontelli (2002) **Twins** – from fetus to child. Routledge.

Lawrence Wright (1997) **Twins** – genes, environment and the mystery of identity. Phoenix.

For more about premature babies see:

Nikki Bradford (2000) **Your Premature baby** 0–5 years. Frances Lincoln.

Sandra Lang (2003) **Breastfeeding special care babies** (2nd ed.) Baillière Tindall.

index

teach yourself®

teach yourself: the range

From Advanced Sudoku to Zulu, you'll find everything you need in the **teach yourself** range, in books, on CD and on DVD.

Visit **www.teachyourself.co.uk** for more details.

Advanced Sudoku and Kakuro
Afrikaans
Alexander Technique
Algebra
Ancient Greek
Applied Psychology
Arabic
Arabic Conversation
Aromatherapy
Art History
Astrology
Astronomy
AutoCAD 2004
AutoCAD 2007
Ayurveda
Baby Massage and Yoga
Baby Signing
Baby Sleep
Bach Flower Remedies
Backgammon
Ballroom Dancing
Basic Accounting
Basic Computer Skills
Basic Mathematics
Beauty
Beekeeping
Beginner's Arabic Script
Beginner's Chinese Script
Beginner's Dutch

Beginner's French
Beginner's German
Beginner's Greek
Beginner's Greek Script
Beginner's Hindi
Beginner's Hindi Script
Beginner's Italian
Beginner's Japanese
Beginner's Japanese Script
Beginner's Latin
Beginner's Mandarin Chinese
Beginner's Portuguese
Beginner's Russian
Beginner's Russian Script
Beginner's Spanish
Beginner's Turkish
Beginner's Urdu Script
Bengali
Better Bridge
Better Chess
Better Driving
Better Handwriting
Biblical Hebrew
Biology
Birdwatching
Blogging
Body Language
Book Keeping
Brazilian Portuguese

Bridge
British Citizenship Test, The
British Empire, The
British Monarchy from Henry VIII, The
Buddhism
Bulgarian
Bulgarian Conversation
Business French
Business Plans
Business Spanish
Business Studies
C++
Calculus
Calligraphy
Cantonese
Caravanning
Car Buying and Maintenance
Card Games
Catalan
Chess
Chi Kung
Chinese Medicine
Christianity
Classical Music
Coaching
Cold War, The
Collecting
Computing for the Over 50s
Consulting
Copywriting
Correct English
Counselling
Creative Writing
Cricket
Croatian
Crystal Healing
CVs
Czech
Danish
Decluttering
Desktop Publishing
Detox
Digital Home Movie Making
Digital Photography
Dog Training

Drawing
Dream Interpretation
Dutch
Dutch Conversation
Dutch Dictionary
Dutch Grammar
Eastern Philosophy
Electronics
English as a Foreign Language
English Grammar
English Grammar as a Foreign Language
Entrepreneurship
Estonian
Ethics
Excel 2003
Feng Shui
Film Making
Film Studies
Finance for Non-Financial Managers
Finnish
First World War, The
Fitness
Flash 8
Flash MX
Flexible Working
Flirting
Flower Arranging
Franchising
French
French Conversation
French Dictionary
French for Homebuyers
French Grammar
French Phrasebook
French Starter Kit
French Verbs
French Vocabulary
Freud
Gaelic
Gaelic Conversation
Gaelic Dictionary
Gardening
Genetics
Geology

German
German Conversation
German Grammar
German Phrasebook
German Starter Kit
German Vocabulary
Globalization
Go
Golf
Good Study Skills
Great Sex
Green Parenting
Greek
Greek Conversation
Greek Phrasebook
Growing Your Business
Guitar
Gulf Arabic
Hand Reflexology
Hausa
Herbal Medicine
Hieroglyphics
Hindi
Hindi Conversation
Hinduism
History of Ireland, The
Home PC Maintenance and
   Networking
How to DJ
How to Run a Marathon
How to Win at Casino Games
How to Win at Horse Racing
How to Win at Online Gambling
How to Win at Poker
How to Write a Blockbuster
Human Anatomy & Physiology
Hungarian
Icelandic
Improve Your French
Improve Your German
Improve Your Italian
Improve Your Spanish
Improving Your Employability
Indian Head Massage
Indonesian
Instant French

Instant German
Instant Greek
Instant Italian
Instant Japanese
Instant Portuguese
Instant Russian
Instant Spanish
Internet, The
Irish
Irish Conversation
Irish Grammar
Islam
Israeli-Palestinian Conflict, The
Italian
Italian Conversation
Italian for Homebuyers
Italian Grammar
Italian Phrasebook
Italian Starter Kit
Italian Verbs
Italian Vocabulary
Japanese
Japanese Conversation
Java
JavaScript
Jazz
Jewellery Making
Judaism
Jung
Kama Sutra, The
Keeping Aquarium Fish
Keeping Pigs
Keeping Poultry
Keeping a Rabbit
Knitting
Korean
Latin
Latin American Spanish
Latin Dictionary
Latin Grammar
Letter Writing Skills
Life at 50: For Men
Life at 50: For Women
Life Coaching
Linguistics
LINUX

Lithuanian	Philosophy of Mind
Magic	Philosophy of Religion
Mahjong	Phone French
Malay	Phone German
Managing Stress	Phone Italian
Managing Your Own Career	Phone Japanese
Mandarin Chinese	Phone Mandarin Chinese
Mandarin Chinese Conversation	Phone Spanish
Marketing	Photography
Marx	Photoshop
Massage	PHP with MySQL
Mathematics	Physics
Meditation	Piano
Middle East Since 1945, The	Pilates
Modern China	Planning Your Wedding
Modern Hebrew	Polish
Modern Persian	Polish Conversation
Mosaics	Politics
Music Theory	Portuguese
Mussolini's Italy	Portuguese Conversation
Nazi Germany	Portuguese for Homebuyers
Negotiating	Portuguese Grammar
Nepali	Portuguese Phrasebook
New Testament Greek	Postmodernism
NLP	Pottery
Norwegian	PowerPoint 2003
Norwegian Conversation	PR
Old English	Project Management
One-Day French	Psychology
One-Day French – the DVD	Quick Fix French Grammar
One-Day German	Quick Fix German Grammar
One-Day Greek	Quick Fix Italian Grammar
One-Day Italian	Quick Fix Spanish Grammar
One-Day Polish	Quick Fix: Access 2002
One-Day Portuguese	Quick Fix: Excel 2000
One-Day Spanish	Quick Fix: Excel 2002
One-Day Spanish – the DVD	Quick Fix: HTML
One-Day Turkish	Quick Fix: Windows XP
Origami	Quick Fix: Word
Owning a Cat	Quilting
Owning a Horse	Recruitment
Panjabi	Reflexology
PC Networking for Small	Reiki
Businesses	Relaxation
Personal Safety and Self Defence	Retaining Staff
Philosophy	Romanian